Praise for *The Assembly*

"Assembly matters. It has always mattered to a people met by God in flesh and in community. Gordon Lathrop, through elegant prose and with compelling vision, helps us remember *how* and *why* assembly matters. In the wake of a pandemic, and in this cultural moment, nothing matters more to Christian mission."

—JAMES FARWELL, professor of liturgy,
Virginia Theological Seminary

"Gordon Lathrop, liturgical, biblical, and confessional scholar, sings the assembly in these pages and invites us into that song to discover the heart of faith, Jesus Christ existing as community. In these engaging pages, Lathrop draws us into the communal body of Christ and the practice of assembly—talking and eating together, and then walking together out in the world, turned toward the neighbor."

—DIRK G. LANGE, assistant general secretary,
Lutheran World Federation

"We have needed this book about the Sunday assembly; it is breathing space and a compass of hope for doing church. Here we receive a wise, gracious, and directive mapping of connections between the physical gathering, its symbols, and, by it, our ongoing reorientation in God's mercy for the life of the world. Gordon W. Lathrop once again gives us a liturgical spirituality that is material, without pretense, here and now and still yearning, at once biblical, theological, and historical, all to renew us again in the communal phenomenon of weekly gathering around the presence of Christ in the assembly."

—JENNIFER LORD, professor of homiletics and liturgical studies, Austin Presbyterian Theological Seminary

"In the present situation, facing a global ecological crisis and in the wake of pandemic, Gordon Lathrop's lucid theological reassessment of the necessity of the assembly and of communal life is just what the church needs."

    Kari Veiteberg, bishop of Oslo, Church of Norway

"Gordon Lathrop offers timely guidance to an ecumenical audience as the churches gather once again in assembly to offer thanksgiving to God and receive invitations for Christian witness in the world. What the reader will discover in this fine work is the wisdom of a pastor, a wisdom that avoids antiquarianism and trendiness, a wisdom born of thoughtful teaching, decades with the assembly, and telling the truth of the gospel. Take up this work: read and reflect and let it shape your care for the assembly."

    Samuel Torvend, university chair in Lutheran studies, emeritus, Pacific Lutheran University

"Like any precious gem, this work deserves to be admired, savored, and viewed from many angles. This book is the work of a seasoned scholar who draws easily and fulsomely from numerous ecumenical sources, from the Bible to contemporary hymn writers. In an era that prizes the 'self,' this book is an invitation to 'become who we are' as members of each other from the font to the grave. It reminds us that in covenant religion no one is alone. This needs to be savored, not just read, and to be lived, not just understood."

    Kevin W. Irwin, professor, The Catholic University of America

The Assembly

THE ASSEMBLY
a spirituality

Gordon W.
Lathrop

FORTRESS PRESS
MINNEAPOLIS

THE ASSEMBLY
A Spirituality

Copyright © 2022 Fortress Press, an imprint of 1517 Media. All rights reserved. Except for brief quotations in critical articles or reviews, no part of this book may be reproduced in any manner without prior written permission from the publisher. Email copyright@1517.media or write to Permissions, Fortress Press, PO Box 1209, Minneapolis, MN 55440-1209.

With the exception of the places where ἐκκλησία in the New Testament is translated as "assembly," the place where Psalm 95 is quoted from the psalter translation in *Evangelical Lutheran Worship* (Minneapolis: Augsburg Fortress, 2006), and the place where 1 Peter 2:9–10 is quoted from *Readings for the Assembly, Cycle A* (Minneapolis: Augsburg Fortress, 1995), all Scripture quotations are from New Revised Standard Version Bible, copyright © 1989 National Council of the Churches of Christ in the United States of America. Used by permission. All rights reserved worldwide.

English translation of the Lord's Prayer, © 1998, English Language Liturgical Consultation (ELLC), and used by permission. www.englishtexts.org.

English translations of the Apostles' Creed and Nicene Creed © 1998, English Language Liturgical Consultation (ELLC), and used by permission. www.englishtexts.org.

Herbert F. Brokering, "Alleluia! Jesus Is Risen!," copyright 1995, Augsburg Fortress; used with permission.

"What Is This Place," copyright © 1967, Gooi en Sticht, text by Huub Oosterhuis, Baarn, The Netherlands. All rights reserved. Exclusive agent for English-language countries: OCP. Used with permission.

Cover image: Paschal candle, Shutterstock / pnmart
Elements in stained glass, Shutterstock

Cover Design: Laurie Ingram Design

Print ISBN: 978-1-5064-7881-4
eBook ISBN: 978-1-5064-7882-1

For
Pastor Thomas G. Christensen,
in thanksgiving
for sixty years of friendship,
and for his care for assemblies
in Cameroon,
Denmark, America, Germany, and France

ἐν τῷ συμπληροῦσθαι τὴν ἡμέραν τῆς πεντηκοστῆς
ἦσαν πάντες ὁμοῦ ἐπὶ τὸ αὐτό
When the day of Pentecost had come,
they were all together in one place.

Acts 2:1

καὶ τῇ τοῦ ἡλίου λεγομένῃ ἡμέρᾳ
πάντων ... ἐπὶ τὸ αὐτὸ συνέλευσις γίνεται
And on the day named after the sun,
all ... are gathered together in one place.

Justin Martyr
1 Apology 67

ᾄδω τὰς ἐκκλησίας
I sing the assemblies

Ignatius of Antioch
to the Magnesians 1:2

Contents

Preface ix

Introduction: Christian Assembly and Liturgical Spirituality 1

Part One: Learning the Assembly by Heart

1. What Is the Assembly? 17
2. Why Is the Assembly Important? 33
3. Why Are the Sacraments Assembly Events? 55
4. How Does the Assembly Form Us for Daily Living? 73

Part Two: A Critical Catechism for the Assembly

5. Catechism and Sacraments: The Purpose of Assembly 91
6. The Lord's Prayer: Assembly, Bread, and Forgiveness Now 105
7. The Creed: Assembly and the Communion of Saints 119
8. The Commandments: Assembly, the Name of God, and the Neighbor 135

Works Cited 151

Index 159

Preface

Fifteen years ago, when I had been a pastor for thirty-seven years and had just retired from full-time teaching and full-time ministry, I wrote a little book about the identity and central tasks of the ordained leader of any public Christian assembly. It was called *The Pastor: A Spirituality*. I hoped for it to be ecumenically accessible and encouraging to pastors, ministers, and priests. In any case, it was my own reflections, my questions, my proposals, my hopes for parish ministry in a difficult time.

But already in that book, I had written, "The most important symbol of Christ in the room is not the minister, not the altar, not even the bread and wine or the water of the font. It is the assembly, the body of Christ, as the New Testament says." I still think that is true. If anything, this recent and painful time of the pandemic, when the wisest and most caring course has been not to assemble at all, has illuminated that conviction and strengthened it. Thus this book turns intentionally to the assembly itself, to formation in assembly practice, to thinking about why and how the assembly is so important in Christianity.

I am writing this book in a more difficult time than was the context for the earlier volume. For many months, during the coronavirus pandemic, pastors of responsible congregations had to work remotely, with little or no in-person contact with their communities. Even more, the assemblies they served had not been meeting or not been meeting fully. That absence brought the reality of what we were missing strongly to our attention. Or it should have. It is true that even before this pandemic, people had been noticing significant declines in assembly attendance, declines that some scholars associated with the loss of community—of "social capital"—in the modern world generally. Robert Putnam, the author of the book *Bowling Alone*, published at the turn of the century, pointed to one major source for this decline: the presence of "virtual community" on television screens in our living rooms and on our computers. That presence became even more striking in the time of quarantine and sheltering in place. Not only for work or school or entertainment but also for church, various electronic resources have become a primary means of communication, enabling virtual meetings. We can be grateful for these means, though one wonders whether assembly, even as it becomes safer, will come back.

But for Christians, from the very beginnings of Christianity, assembly has been essential. One old North African deacon in the early fourth century, accused by the Roman magistrate of illegally enabling Christians to meet on Sunday in his home, said simply, "We cannot live, we cannot be, without that meeting."

This book is intended as an ecumenical exploration of that assertion. More, in the hope of the ongoing restoration of in-the-body assembly among us, the book seeks to outline a communal spirituality that will treasure, support, and continually seek to renew the Christian assembly. If the earlier book was about the pastor or presider who serves assemblies, this book focuses on the identity of the meeting itself.

There is no need to have read *The Pastor* to be able to read this book. In fact, this writing, while it will be shaped much as that book was shaped, is intended for a different audience: all the participants in the assembly themselves, including their appointed leaders. My hope is that it will be experienced as hopeful and encouraging, a deep breath as we have begun to meet again, a rationale for the coming years when we once again can breathe in one another's presence and get on with the assembly's work. We have before us the task of reclaiming and valuing the assembly, and this book hopes to help. If you are a participant in an assembly, the book is for you.

Still, if you are a leader in a Christian assembly, I do hope that you will find this book to be in dialogue with *The Pastor*. And I hope that reading them side by side may be helpful to you.

Of course, the book has an author. I am a Lutheran Christian who is also a pastor and a liturgist. That will be clear especially in the instances and images from my own experience—in which I use the first-person singular—that are printed in italics and set in counterpoint to the main body of the text. You may choose to skip these passages, but you do need to know that this is the person who is writing this book. Nonetheless, since all Christians have assemblies, I am hoping that the main body of the text will indeed be ecumenically accessible.

That text will proceed by first, in an introduction, considering definitions: In what sense is assembly a symbol? What do we mean by "spirituality," and can it be communal? And what is "worship" or "liturgy," the matters that seem to be the principal work of assemblies? Then, in part 1, we will turn to the most basic questions of this spirituality: What is assembly? Why does it matter? Why are the sacraments assembly events? And how does the assembly form us to live in our daily lives? Finally, in part 2, we will consider how "assembly" shows up in all the texts of the "catechism"—the Ten Commandments, the Apostles' Creed, the Lord's Prayer, and the basic texts of the sacraments—texts that are given us in baptism and so belong to baptismal living. What can that catechism use mean for living in and from the assembly?

Thought about assemblies, as we will see, has a long history. Among Lutherans since the sixteenth century, the primary definition of "church" has been "the assembly of all believers among whom the gospel is purely preached and the holy sacraments are administered according to the gospel" (Augsburg Confession VII). That idea can be seen visually presented in the sixteenth-century altarpiece painting that still stands in St. Mary's Church in the heart of Wittenberg, Germany, the "mother church" of the Lutheran movement (one way to see this image is to search for *Cranach Altarpiece Wittenberg* on the internet), where crowds of ordinary people are shown as gathered around preaching and the sacraments, and those crowds spill off the edge of the paintings as if to suggest that we too are included. We will need to think about those strong centers of the meeting and that inclusive crowd as we consider what assembly is.

But assembly is both much older and much more recent than sixteenth-century examples. Robert Hovda, an important twentieth-century Roman Catholic liturgist, once wrote, "Among the symbols with which liturgy deals, none is more important than this assembly of believers." We will seek to think about that symbol.

And Julian of Norwich, a fifteenth-century anchoress who lived for years alone in a cell attached to a church—while plague, for much of that time, was raging in her city—still knew about assembly: she had a window that opened into the church itself so that she could see and hear the gathering and receive communion. She also had another window, open to the world, so that she could give help to others. More, she powerfully imagined her linkage to those other people, those comembers of the body of Christ, writing in her "Vision Showed to a Devout Woman," "Alle that I saye of myselfe, I meene in the persone of alle mine evencristene" (6:1). "All my evenchristians"—such a remarkable expression. Julian, a dedicated solitary, gives us a stunning way to begin to consider the spirituality of assembly. During this pandemic, I have thought of her a lot. I have joined her in being necessarily isolated while wishing I had something like her two windows. I have hoped nonetheless to understand myself as deeply linked to fellow Christians, carrying something of that linkage in my own body. But even more, I am hoping to come back to assembly and to its mission, as if I could at last climb through those windows. We will think about our evenchristians and both of those windows in an assembly-related spirituality.

And there is yet another old articulator of the assembly, this one from the second century: Ignatius of Antioch, a Syrian bishop who was arrested and taken in chains to Rome, where—becoming one of the earliest martyrs—he was killed. But on his way, he was able to write several powerful letters to churches (to assemblies!) mostly in cities in Asia Minor, present-day Turkey. To the assembly in the city of Magnesia on the river Maeander, he wrote, "Knowing the great orderliness of your love towards God I gladly determined to address you in the faith of Jesus Christ. For being counted worthy to bear a most godly name I sing the assemblies in the bonds which I carry about, and pray that in them there may be a union of the flesh and spirit of Jesus Christ, who is our everlasting life" (Ign. *Magn.* 1:1–2a). As we are able to meet again, may there indeed be a union of the flesh and the spirit of Jesus Christ, of our flesh as body of Christ and the Spirit poured out from his death and resurrection. And in our own difficult time, our own bonds, may we all in our lives join Ignatius in singing the assemblies.

So here is one song from one singer, one proposal. Call it simply *The Assembly*. And subtitle it *A Spirituality*. I hope it may be helpful for you as you care about your assembly.

Parts of chapters 2 and 4 appeared in another form as "Assembly: A Biblical-Liturgical Reality We Will Need Again," in *Worship* 95 (April 2021): 129–47. Parts of chapter 4 also appeared in another form as "Thinking Again about Assembly in a Time of Pandemic," in *CrossAccent: Journal of the Association of Lutheran Church Musicians* 28, no. 2 (Summer 2020): 9–17. My thanks are due to the editors of those journals, Bernadette Gasslein and Chad Fothergill, for their graciousness in allowing me to use those articles in this book.

I owe a significant debt of gratitude to Mitzi Budde and to the Bishop Payne Library at the Virginia Theological Seminary where she is head librarian. That collection and her assistance were invaluable.

My deep thanks also go to Scott Tunseth of Fortress Press and to Samuel Torvend, James Farwell, Kevin Irwin, Gail Ramshaw, and the members of the Washington, DC, group of the North American Academy of Liturgy for conversation about and support of this project.

Gordon W. Lathrop

Introduction

Christian Assembly and Liturgical Spirituality

Our gathering with other Christians in a participatory meeting constitutes the most basic symbol of Christianity. That coming together in assembly—coming together, especially on Sunday, with the purpose of reading the Scriptures, hearing their meaning proclaimed, praying for others, and keeping the eucharist—itself constitutes this symbol. We cannot finally have Christianity without it. There certainly have been Christian believers who have had to endure long periods of time alone. But even then, they have remembered these gatherings and longed to come to them again. The elder John, the author of the Revelation at the end of the Christian Bible, was in exile on an island—presumably quite alone—and yet on Sunday, "in the spirit," he found himself called by the risen Christ to be in touch with seven such assemblies (Rev 1:9–11), to imagine them, to write to them, to comfort them, to admonish them. Even the exile lives with this basic gift and mark of Christians.

In our day, such gatherings practice a great variety of other symbols: the holy books opened and read; symbolic language recited and sung; a preacher speaking in biblical images to invite us again to faith; fire, water, and oil blessed and used; bread and wine set out at the center of a communal thanksgiving and then eaten and drunk; symbols painted on the wall or worked into fabrics or glass. The list could go on. But all those symbolic practices depend, first of all, on having a gathering of people to do them or a gathering place to be marked by them. The basic symbol is the meeting itself. We call that meeting "the assembly."

Assembly as Symbol

But how is it a symbol? If a symbol is *a means for communal encounter with larger meaning* or *a thing that enables participation in that to which it refers,* then it is clear how the bread and wine or the holy book are symbols. The Book both stands for the word of God and, when it is read, enables us to receive that Word. The Bread and Cup of the holy communion "proclaim the Lord's death until he comes" (1 Cor 11:26), but they also enable us to eat and drink together the gifts from that death, Christ's body and blood, his presence, and his life.

But what about assembly? To what does it refer? In what does it enable participation?

The Bible is full of descriptions of and hope for a group of people called "the people of God," a group that is seen as responsible to bear witness to God's mercy for the sake of the life of the whole world. The story of Israel recounts such hope; the people of the Jews are, in the first place, that holy people. But the First Letter of Peter, in the New Testament, borrows language that was first used about Israel to describe also the Christian church, as if Christians are being grafted into the vocation of Israel: "You are a chosen race, a royal priesthood, a holy nation, God's own people, in order that you may proclaim the mighty acts of the one who called you out of darkness into the marvelous light of God. Once you were not a people, but now you are God's people; once you had not received mercy, but now you have received mercy" (1 Pet 2:9–10). The Christian assembly points to that people. More, joining an assembly enables actual participation in this people who are being made people of God, actual reception of such mercy, and actual witness-bearing to God's mighty acts for the sake of the life of the world. Assembly enables our communal encounter with this larger meaning, sets out a symbol for the holy people that also draws us into its reality.

But the symbol is more profound yet. The apostle Paul, counseling unity in diversity, called the gathering of Christians at Corinth "the body of Christ" (1 Cor 12:27). He repeated the image in writing to the Romans (Rom 12:4–5). He clearly meant to so designate the other such gatherings elsewhere and then the whole church in all the world as a great gathering. After Paul, the Letters to the Ephesians and to the Colossians used the same name for the church (Col 1:18, 24; 2:19; 3:15; Eph 1:23; 3:6; 4:4, 12, 16). By such an understanding, the assembly is a symbol for Jesus Christ. If a "body" enables the presence of a person and encounter with that presence, then for Paul and those after him, the assembly signs the presence of the risen Christ and enables the encounter with him. Indeed, as if the gathering were a corporate person, this symbol draws us into and makes us part of "Christ existing as community," as Dietrich Bonhoeffer wrote in his *Sanctorum Communio*. Since the German word Bonhoeffer used for "community" was *Gemeinde*, the ordinary German word for "congregation" or "assembly," we could translate this to "Christ existing as assembly."

But we need to be careful here. Saying that the assembly is a symbol of the people of God and a sign of Christ can lead us to think that it must be a perfect society. Far from it. Idealizing the church can be one of our worst mistakes. We need to remember that all of the symbols that Christians exercise are unique in character. They carry within themselves their own critique. They always express their meaning by paradox. Thus in my earlier book, *The Pastor*, this passage occurred:

> The symbols that live at the heart of Christian life are a specific sort of symbol. The sacred words of the Scripture, their collection together into a significant book, and the practice of their holy reading in an assembly might suggest that here we will receive glorious, shimmering, world-making myths, the deeds of mighty figures, words that take us out of this world simply in the hearing. But, in fact, these are stories and poems of ordinary and needy people, of sin and death and loss and hope in this world, and of the passion and anger and surprising mercy of God in dealing with these people. They are words that have room for us, in this world. Such is the Christian holy book. Furthermore, the meal that we keep, in its intensity and focus, its staple food and festive drink, its ceremonial welcome of a wide circle, might suggest that we are consuming magical food, food of the angels, a heavenly banquet, food that will grant us

immortality. Then we hear the content of the feast: "the body of Christ, the blood of Christ, given for you." A specific, real death is proclaimed, and if "immortality" is given, then this is a new kind of freedom from death, coming in a world-affirming, bounded, palpable and mortal way, *here*. More: . . . This saving bath that joins us to the holy assembly is an act that identifies us with the crucified Jesus Christ and so with all those with whom he identifies: the little, neglected, oppressed, poor, dying, sinful, marginal ones of the world. These symbols enable participation in the wonderful things to which they refer only by taking us to a place we had not expected, gathering us around a thing we thought far away from meaning and hope, inviting us to faith. They are all *broken symbols*—powerful still in their reference, in the hope they evoke, but made up of the unexpected, the ordinary, the failed, the equivocal rather than the absolute—made up of the *cross*. These broken symbols gather us—our deepest hopes, our very selves—into the circles of their reference, but then they lead us not to possession or control but to *faith*.

These enacted but broken symbols are at the heart of the meeting of Christians. They are what the assembly does.

Just so, if the assembly itself is a symbol, that symbol needs to be understood as broken. This holy assembly enlivened by the Holy Spirit is a gathering of the needy and the sinful. There is room in it for us and not just our dreams of perfect community—and not just our friends or people like us either.

After all, when Paul wrote about the assembly being the body of Christ, he was addressing the church at Corinth or at Rome, both groups—as his letters make clear—being marked by disputes, divisions, failures, and mistakes. And when the Gospel according to Matthew uses images for the church in parables—a field planted with wheat, a net thrown into the sea, or guests come to a wedding banquet (Matt 13:24–30, 47–50; 22:1–14)—there are good and bad fish in that net, weeds among the wheat in the field, and good and bad guests filling the wedding hall. Deciding who is good and who is bad is never, ever up to us. Indeed, we all are a kind of mixture. More, the holy people of Israel in the Old Testament, the people called to be a people of priests for the world, are again and again—in the narratives and in the words of the prophets—described as complaining, failing, misunderstanding, sinning. As the Christian assemblies share with Israel the vocation of witness to the world, they also share in such histories of failure and yet hope. The very First Letter of Peter, the source of the text that shows the assemblies as symbols of the people of God, is full of exhortations and fierce counsel, counsel that would not have been needed were the assemblies perfect societies.

We may take comfort—even joy—at this news. The assembly about which we want to think here does not need to be a place of pretense. It needs to be seen as real, made up of real people in a real world: bodies of flesh and blood, children and adults, youth and the aged and those in between, breathing side by side, with their genuine hopes and deep failings.

But we find out who they together are not by looking at their individual identities nor by asking them to look at themselves. Instead, we look with them to Christ giving himself away to them in word and sacrament so that they might in turn give to their neighbor. In those gifts, the Spirit poured out from the death and resurrection of Jesus makes them the body of Christ; that is their identity. In this very gathering, the holy Trinity shows them mercy, calling this "not a people" to be the very holy people of God; that is their identity.

A Paradoxical Communal Spirituality

But then we have come to "spirituality" as we want to think about it here.

Spirituality, most commonly in our culture, is thought about as an individual matter, the way one person accesses and lives with matters of "spirit." And those matters of spirit are most often thought to be more or less private and away from earthly, material life: private prayers; a personal and interior relationship with the divine; ideals, dreams, visions; heavenly realities and angelic beings; life beyond death.

Not here. *Christian* spirituality may be best conceived as a communal undertaking. It came about in the first place because of what happened to a group of people when they encountered the death and resurrection of Jesus. A real, material event lives at the heart of this encounter. Jesus did exist, he did teach, and he was killed. Christians then came to believe that especially in assembly, they still encountered him. Indeed, that encounter frequently upended and reversed what was thought to be religious or spiritual, and it did so from the beginning. The New Testament contains a developing record of that surprising rereading of religious categories: the Messiah is a crucified man; "Spirit" is the life that flows to a community from this crucified one; God is found where religion thought God could not be; sinners are welcome first in the dominion of this God. At least some Christians even came to see this further reversal of what is ordinarily expected in religion: in Christ there is neither Jew nor Greek, slave nor free, male nor female. And enacted in assembly, all those broken symbols we have considered bore continual witness to grace abounding for sinners and the needy.

This upending has continued. Christians still believe that they encounter the crucified and risen Jesus Christ, especially in assembly. And as Rowan Williams writes, Christian spirituality involves the ongoing history of communal encounters with the religious reversals that take place because of Christ. Christian spirituality embraces paradoxes, matters that seem to contain their own contradiction but are nonetheless so true that they illumine the world. Led by a crucified man who is alive and formed by a baptismal immersion into death that makes us alive together, Christians find their assemblies also to be paradoxical. For example, when those assemblies are faithful, they are strongly centered yet open, profoundly communal yet always personal, filled with our participatory action yet trusting that the primary actor is God.

The Centered Open Assembly

Christian assemblies are not just any meeting; they are meetings that have a clear and accented center: the presence of Jesus Christ in word and sacrament, in prayer, and in the very gathering itself. Making that center clear and unobstructed, making the symbols that carry that center to be large and beautiful: these tasks continually constitute the renewal to which these assemblies are called.

"Write the vision; make it plain on tablets, so that a runner may read it," says the prophet (Hab 2:2), and the assembly is to do the same with the vision that lives in the Word and Bath and Table at its heart. Yet while one might think that such centering would carry along a necessary creation of boundaries—"this place is only for those who already understand and identify with the center"—this is not the case. The Jesus Christ of the Gospels, the one at the center, identifies again and again with the outsider, the compromised, the sinner. In his cross, he is among the unclean. When we come to him, we are directed toward those others, united with those others. A pastor who presides attentively in this assembly, being charged especially with caring for and serving the center of the assembly, will also have a heart for the person who is only tentatively in the room, the person in the back row who seems ready to leave. A gathering that is glad to be together around such a center will also repeatedly be glad to welcome the stranger.

Of course, this does not always happen, maybe not even most of the time. Devoted Christian communities are still real social entities that inevitably create their own boundaries. But the content of the center itself, the movement of God in Christ toward the needy world, will always press the assembly toward reform. "Strong center, open door" is one way to articulate the continually reformed assembly. And that dictum means an open door both for going out in witness and service and for coming in with our need, all of us beggars for mercy.

The Personal Communal Assembly

The very idea of Christian assembly being a corporate person— "Christ existing as assembly" or "the body of Christ"—means this gathering is communal. But we are wrong if we think that "communal" means "impersonal." Each person there should be treasured, honored, respected, beginning with the least member of the body. An attentive presider will embody such honoring. So will an attentive participant in the congregation. This assembly ought not be a crowd engaged in "groupthink." If it is a crowd, Jesus Christ in the center of the assembly is also calling to each one, addressing each one. Yet it ought not also be simply a collection of individuals. Our current society privileges the individual in competition. Here the individual is called to be part of the body, honoring and serving the others. The late medieval and Enlightenment seating patterns in European churches, where governmental figures or royal persons were given higher or closer places, were thus a denial of the deep identity of the assembly. So is now the modern dream of intimacy in any group, as if our leaders have direct access to our deepest feelings, indeed as if we all should have and should allow such access to one another. For example, a preacher may walk up and down the aisle, speaking familiarly into the faces of the congregation, perhaps calling some by name. Or a greeter at the door may expect you to tell what your week has been like. In both cases, the leader seems to be reaching for immediacy, for direct relationship with the other.

But Dietrich Bonhoeffer was right to argue in *Life Together* that in a healthy community, there is no such immediacy. Access to the other person in the Christian assembly is always best mediated by symbols of Christ: the formal and ritual gesture of the peace of Christ; the shared communion bread put carefully into each hand; our sung participation, side by side, in a common hymn; the preacher standing in the assembly at the place of the book, speaking to all in such a way that each one is addressed; a deep bow exchanged at the mutual greeting between presider and assembly before prayer; the laying on of hands at a blessing done with respect and dignity. These symbols come far deeper in mutual exchange between persons than does the current ready reaching for the soul of the other. Thus work on stronger common symbols in our liturgies will likewise be work on a stronger presence of the paradox of the personal communal assembly.

The Participatory Receptive Assembly

A primary goal of the twentieth- and twenty-first-century liturgical renewal in all of our churches has been the full active participation of all of the faithful in the mystery of Christ. We continue to work toward that goal. The liturgy is sung and spoken in the vernacular, and work continues on constantly revising and updating that language so that people may fully speak and sing with understanding and with all their hearts. The presider faces the assembly, intending to draw all into the prayer. Many people help lead us—readers, singers, communion ministers, doorkeepers, leaders of prayer—many of them laypeople and all of them standing for the whole assembly, assisting the whole assembly. Choirs seek to understand themselves primarily not as a concert group to whom the rest of us then simply listen but as the rehearsed voices of the assembly, helping us all to sing. The principal musician of the assembly thus is not simply the "organist" or "choirmaster" but the *cantor*, the leader of assembly song. Especially intercessions and eucharistic prayers have been freshly drafted so that the assembly responds, everyone engaging in the bids and in the thanksgiving.

But all of this participation has been intended to be participation in "the mystery of Christ," which is at the same time the mystery of the presence of the holy Trinity. Christians believe that the primary actor in the room is indeed the holy Trinity: such is the mystery. The Holy Spirit has drawn us together and enlivens our singing and empowers our sacraments. God speaks in the reading and preaching of the Scripture and in the song that responds. Jesus Christ stands with the whole assembly as it prays in his name. It is the risen Christ who greets us in peace as we greet one another. This same Jesus Christ gives himself away in the holy supper. On, in, and under all the participation here, "the grace of the Lord Jesus Christ, the love of God, and the communion of the Holy Spirit" (2 Cor 13:13) has been with us all. The blessing of this same triune God sends us away, turning us toward the needs of the world and the specific needs of our neighbors. Thus, paradoxically, the fully active assembly is, exactly at the same time, profoundly receptive, receiving all that comes with the presence and gift of God.

In what follows in this book, we will be exploring what such a shared spirituality of centered openness, personal communality, and receptive participation means as we recover and renew our assemblies. But first we need to think further about how this spirituality is a *liturgical spirituality*. What is liturgy? And how is it the work of the assembly?

Rehearsing the Symbols

In its meeting, the centered, open assembly—the personal communal assembly, the participatory receptive assembly, the gathering of needy sinners that is the holy people—enacts a series of symbols. It is itself a symbol. And the enacting of all these symbols makes up its work.

We have called that enacting by a variety of names. We have said that we come together to *worship*. But that is not quite right. We do indeed sing praise and give thanks to God, reciting the "mighty acts" of God. But that is by no means all we do in the meeting. We also baptize or remember baptism, read the Scriptures and hear them proclaimed, pray for the needs of the world, greet one another with peace, set the table and eat and drink, and are sent for witness and service, sent to give help to others. Christians can and do worship anywhere, not only in the assembly. But they enact these central, communal symbols only when they gather.

We have also said that we come together to do the *service*. This could be interesting, remembering what we said about the participatory, receptive assembly. On, in, and under our acts—our serving God and one another—*God* acts, *God* serves. Indeed, a basic theology of the Christian meeting would say that the triune God is coming out toward us—in the cross and resurrection of Christ but also in the Spirit drawing us together into Christ—but, even more, going out toward the needy world. God serves us with mercy so that we might turn in mercy toward our neighbors, following where God in Christ has gone before us. The problem is that we do not easily hear all that meaning in the simple term the *service*. Perhaps we should, but we do not. Such astonishing meaning needs to be taught.

It might be better to say we come to do the *liturgy*. That word especially works if we remember that *liturgy* originally meant a public work for the benefit of the people. The only problem is that in its original Greek setting, that public work—like someone paying for a series of dramas or for a festival in an ancient Greek city—was usually done by one or two wealthy people for the sake of the whole community. And when the same word was used in the Septuagint, the primary Greek translation of the Hebrew Scriptures, it was then used for the cultic activity of the priests in the tabernacle or temple. Neither use is right for what the assembly does all together, participating in its action. Perhaps the word works if we recall that, as 1 Peter has it, we are all those priests and the "cultic activity" we are engaged in is not giving something to God but receiving God's mercy so that we can then turn to our neighbor. Or the word might work if we think that all of us are those "wealthy people," wealthy with the astonishing mercy of God, and the public work we are all doing together is prayer and then sending and being sent for the life of the world. Such a liturgical spirituality will be the continually renewed and surprising discovery that we are all doing this public work and, ultimately, doing it for others. Christian liturgy will then be its own upending of the old religious practice of cultic acts in the temple, the reversal of the old civic practice of donated public works.

But perhaps the best thing to say is simply "we go to church" or even, using a common African American Christian idiom, "we do church" or "we have church." Then our words for the event point profoundly to the assembly itself and to the assembly as an event. Whatever we call it, the meeting comes together to carry out a series of central symbols and thus to be itself a symbol. The work of the assembly is the enacting of the symbols.

In what follows in this book, we will be considering how our common life as Christians can be shaped by those symbols—both the word and sacraments at the heart of the meeting and the symbolic character of the meeting itself. We will thus be exploring a liturgical spirituality. In the first part of the book, we will be asking these questions: What is assembly? Why does it matter? Why are the sacraments assembly events? And how does the assembly form us to live in our daily lives? In doing this, we will be exploring the symbols, their practice, and their meaning. But because the classic confessional texts of Christian faith are also called "symbols," our weighing the effect of symbols on our liturgical spirituality will, in the second part of the book, go further still: What do the sabbath commandment in the Ten Commandments, the mention of the church in the Creed and of bread and forgiveness in the Lord's Prayer, and the biblical meaning of the sacraments have to do with assembly?

Rehearsing the symbols—going over what they are and what they mean, considering them, and actually doing them—belongs to the rediscovery and the practice of a spirituality of the assembly.

* * *

I remember how profoundly important it was for me to discover the story of Emeritus when reading a book about the meaning of Sunday by the Swiss Reformed scholar Willi Rordorf. Emeritus was that early fourth-century North African deacon who was arrested in the last great persecution of Christians, ordered by the emperor Diocletian. Emeritus was accused of allowing Christians to meet in his home, and that accusation ultimately led to his execution. His response when he was brought before the magistrate is reported to have been "Sine dominico non possumus." Dominicum means, more or less, "the matter or the thing of the Lord." So "without the Lord's thing, it is not possible for us." It may be that Emeritus was saying, "We cannot exist without the Lord's Supper." Or maybe, "Without the meeting on the Lord's Day"—the Lord's meeting, thus—"we cannot be." Probably he intended both, "Lord's day" (Rev 1:10) and "Lord's supper" (1 Cor 11:20) being New Testament expressions for the time and the content of the Christian meeting. In any case, Emeritus was willing to die for that meeting.

I hope to be like Emeritus, though I do not know if I have the courage. I do know that I am a Christian only because of that meeting, because there is such a thing as the Christian assembly. Not, by any means, because all of the meetings of the Christian assembly that I have known have been so wonderful. The meeting Emeritus was enabling may not have been so wonderful either. But the classic content of the meeting—the word and the sacraments celebrated there, the symbols set next to one another and profoundly reinterpreting the world, the mercy of God making use of those symbols, a community made and commissioned by those symbols—is everything to me. I think we live from the assembly of the church. I have come to believe and trust in God again and again because of that assembly. I have been rightly turned toward the needy world there. And in that meeting, gathered into the presence of Christ, I am made part of that "we," that "us," of which Emeritus speaks.

Say it again: Sine dominico non possumus.

Another author who has written about the assembly and has also mattered to me is Nikolai Grundtvig—a fascinating nineteenth-century Danish poet, scholar, pastor, and bishop—who described the assembly in an article about the ongoing value of the Lutheran Reformation. The Reformation would be complete and the church in good order, he said, *when bishops stand at the altar table, "truly representing the Good Shepherd who lays down his life for the sheep"; pastors stand at the baptismal bath "as Zion's watchers in the power of the Spirit"; and the people of God let the light they have seen at both shine forth in the world. More, that good order calls for "the learned" to watch over the book of the Bible in the light of what happens in the eucharist and "to watch that the church has open doors for going out as well as for coming in."*

I want the assembly to have such pastors and bishops and scholars serving the purpose of the meeting. I join Grundtvig in wanting to read the Bible in the light of Christ's giving himself away at the table. I also want to help it be seen that the church needs open doors—for everyone in need freely to come in but also for all of us to go out again toward a needy world. I hope this book serves the purpose of those doors. In Grundtvig's sense, doors are a fine symbol of the assembly, representing its open and centered gathering and also its personal and communal sending.

Another such symbol is the paschal candle. One is represented burning on the cover of this book. Lit first—in assemblies that use this candle—to proclaim the resurrection at the outset of the great Vigil of Easter, it burns during all fifty days of Easter and so at the heart of every year but also at every baptism and every remembrance of baptism and every funeral. It stands for the risen Christ in the midst of the assembly. More, it stands for Jesus Christ existing as assembly, as the one who is both at the center and at the periphery of the gathering, the one who anchors the community yet addresses each person in love, the one who acts underneath and through all of us participating. I hope this book reflects the light of that candle.

Part One

Learning the Assembly by Heart

1

What Is the Assembly?

Perhaps it is like this: The room slowly fills. People are coming into the room past the baptismal font. Some are touching the water and making the sign of the cross on their foreheads or on the upper parts of their bodies. A few adults trace such a cross on the foreheads of their children. Some have brought food to give away, and they place that in a basket near the font. These people all began coming some time ago, when they rose from sleep or rose from their breakfast tables, when they decided "let's go to church," or when they simply dressed to do what they always do on Sundays. But at last, they come together, finding a place to sit in a pattern arranged before a prominent reading desk they can see and a gracious table that seems almost to reach out into their midst. Candles burn to mark these central places. They are glad to be there, in that room, still remembering a painful time when they could not gather in such a group. They are a diverse company: old and middle-aged, young and very young; well dressed and not so well dressed; men and women and non-binary people; laborers and scholars and merchants and the retired; of many skin colors and from different cultures; able-bodied and not so able-bodied. There is some buzz of greeting and quiet conversation in the room that then falls into silence. A bell rings and, as they are able, they all stand, turning to face that font. A vested presider leads them in remembering the baptism that made them part of this group. Then music begins and they all sing as several members of the group, clothed amply in the white that also recalls baptism, follow a cross and a great book that lead them—and with them the presider—to the center or the front of the room. Formal and mutual liturgical greetings follow, then more singing, then a gathering prayer, and they sit to hear the Scripture. They have gathered as the assembly.

Such is "the Gathering," the first part of the four-part ecumenical Sunday liturgy that marks most Christian assemblies. So start here: Who has gathered? Or what has come into being by that gathering? More, what do we actually mean by "the assembly"? What is its history? Is it in the Bible? How has the idea of such a gathering figured in Christian theology and liturgical practice? Can it mean those same things to us today when we join such a gathering?

And further, can we learn the meaning and practice of assembly "by heart"? That is, can it matter so much to us that we find it deeply inscribed in our lives, marking our days, shaping the way we are with others, intimately belonging to how we are Christians, and, at least partly, organizing the way we see the world around us? Can we see again how important—even urgent—this gathering is? These questions can draw us into the possibilities of a spirituality of the assembly.

Assembly in the Bible

A place to begin is in one of the earliest writings of the New Testament, Paul's letter to the Galatians. In Galatians 1:2, Paul addresses this fiercely reforming reassertion of the gospel "to the assemblies of Galatia," or to the "churches of Galatia," as we usually translate the plural of the Greek word *ekklesia*. "Assembly" or "convocation" or even "meeting" or "gathering" are more accurate translations, "church" being an anglicized form of the largely post–New Testament Greek word *kyriakon*, which means "belonging to the Lord." What Paul is talking about is not buildings but events, groups of people who come together in a local place, often someone's house. And in Galatia, they were plural; there were many local assemblies in that region of Asia Minor. As we look further in Galatians and then elsewhere in Paul's writings, we discover that the plurality in Galatia was echoed in many other places. There were assemblies in Judea (Gal 1:22), Paul says, and in Macedonia (2 Cor 8:1). "The assemblies of Asia" (1 Cor 16:19) send greetings to "the assembly of God that is in Corinth" (1 Cor 1:2). All the assemblies among the Gentiles give thanks for Prisca and Aquila (Rom 16:4). Indeed, there is an assembly in the house of Prisca and Aquila

(Rom 16:5; 1 Cor 16:19), as are there assemblies in the house of Philemon (Phlm 2) and, probably much later, in the house of Nympha (Col 4:15). All of the greetings in chapter 16 of Romans most likely point to a diversity of house assemblies in Rome, and then Paul says, "Greet one another with a holy kiss. All the assemblies of Christ greet you" (Rom 16:16). We could go on, naming particular assemblies in particular places as they are mentioned throughout the Pauline correspondence and then also in subsequent passages of the New Testament.

But in the very same passage of Galatians that begins with the address to the assemblies of Galatia and mentions the assemblies of Judea, Paul also writes that he had been "violently persecuting the assembly of God" (Gal 1:13). That global singular is also echoed elsewhere in Paul (e.g., 1 Cor 10:32). And it is probably in reference to this whole "church"—all the assemblies as one great assembly—that Paul speaks of "the Jerusalem above" that is free (Gal 4:26) and, at the end of Galatians, says, "Peace be upon . . . the Israel of God" (Gal 6:16).

Thus the New Testament uses its term—the *assembly*—primarily for a group that has its local gathering in a local place, a group of people thus able to talk together, eat together, and greet one another with a kiss. That is clearly its meaning in passages in which someone's house is mentioned. It is the meaning implied by Paul's anger when the rich exclude the poor from the common meal, thereby "not discerning the body" (1 Cor 11:29). It also seems to be the meaning in one passage of the only Gospel book that uses the word, the instructions to the church in Matthew 18 (see 18:17), in which a process for personal, face-to-face reconciliation in a local group is outlined.

But that is not the word's only usage. It could be that expressions like "the assembly of God that is in Corinth" (1 Cor 1:2) or "the assembly in Ephesus" (Rev 2:1) point to a common, shared identity for several house churches in the city and its environs. More, as we have seen in Galatians, the New Testament also occasionally speaks of all Christians, in every place, as *ekklesia*—"church" or "assembly"—using the singular noun. Similarly, using body and building metaphors for the whole of the Christian movement, post-Pauline writings could call Christ the "head of the body, the assembly" (Col 1:18), and the Matthean Jesus could say, "On this rock I will build my assembly" (Matt 16:18). Again, the nouns are singular.

Although only Matthew uses the name *ekklesia*, recent study of all the Gospels makes clear that they were written for such assemblies. Mark has a clear image of such an assembly, gathered in a house in Galilee, in the very center of the book (Mark 9:33–37). Then the circular structure of this Gospel makes it clear that the conclusion of the book sends us to such an assembly, an assembly where the risen Christ can be seen in the reception of the disregarded little ones, in a serving leadership, and in the account of Christ's death. The other Gospels, all of which made extensive use of Mark, continue to make this point, but they do it by having their image of the continuing assembly of the church as the final rather than the middle passage of each book. In Matthew, it is the assembly of disciples sent to teach and baptize (Matt 28:16–20). In Luke, it is the little Emmaus assembly gathered around the risen Christ known in the interpreted Scripture and the shared meal, and then it is the larger meal assembly to which the Emmaus disciples return (Luke 24:13–49). And in John, it is two Sunday gatherings, the very beginning of week-after-week Sunday gatherings that come down to our time, in which the risen Christ is encountered, the Spirit poured out, the peace shared, and the Gospel book itself treasured (John 20:19–31). These endings make clear that the books themselves have been written for such assemblies, that assembly is the home of the Gospel book, and that our own gatherings are called to hear—even to be *reformed* to hear—what the Gospels say.

There has been a scholarly debate over the source of the Christian use of the word *ekklesia*. Some regard it as borrowed from the Greek political term for the gathering of all the voters in a city, convoked by a crier. They can point to the fact that the term was occasionally used for other associations or *collegia* rather than strictly Christian groups. Indeed, a number of scholars have proposed that the social life of Hellenistic cities and towns in the time of Christian origins—and well into the early centuries of Christian existence—was marked by diverse interest groups, supper clubs, *collegia*, or associations. One minority example of such meetings would have been the Christian gatherings we call "house churches." The various Hellenistic associations, nearly ubiquitous in the ancient Mediterranean world, were neighborhood groups, professional or trade groups, cult groups, ethnic groups, and extended family groups. They were called by a variety of names: associations, societies, guilds, initiates, synagogues, and sometimes, though infrequently, even *ekklesiai*. That may be one possible source.

But other scholars are more inclined to see the background of the Christian use of the word *ekklesia* in the Greek translation of the Hebrew word *qahal*, the principal word used for the "assembly of the Lord" or the "whole assembly of Israel," as found in many places in the Hebrew Scriptures. That proposal does not need to exclude the Greek societal origin: Christian gatherings occupied the same social place as many other Hellenistic house groups and *collegia*. But what they were *called* could well have also had a biblical origin and carried biblical connotations. The comments of Richard Hays about the way Paul read the Old Testament matter here: "Paul's interpretation of Scripture is always a pastoral, community forming activity. . . . He finds in Scripture a rich source of image and metaphor that enables him to declare with power what God is doing in his own time. He reads the Bible neither as a historian nor as a systematic theologian but as a poetic preacher who discerns analogical correspondences between the scriptural story and the gospel that he proclaims." More, Hays writes, "We find Paul calling his readers and hearers to a conversion of the imagination. He was calling Gentiles to understand their identity anew in the light of the gospel of Jesus Christ. . . . Such a thoroughgoing conversion could be fostered and sustained only by a continuous process of bringing the community's beliefs and practices into critical confrontation with the gospel story."

Among those analogical correspondences, those reborn images, those critical calls to a reconfigured identity, we should see the primary name Paul uses to speak of the local assemblies he was addressing. Indeed, it is most likely Paul *himself* who privileges this name for those Christian communities, which otherwise might have been much like other Hellenistic supper clubs and like-minded associations. And his privileging of this name had a reforming, pastoral intent. Paul's extensive use of the word—sometimes in the plural for the various assemblies; sometimes in the singular for one local house gathering or several gatherings in a city; and sometimes in the singular for all the assemblies together as one great worldwide assembly of God—recalls a biblical image. Again, the word is the Greek translation for the Hebrew word *qahal*, the assembly of all Israel as convoked by God, specifically as it was constituted before God at Sinai and again at Jerusalem's Water Gate in the return from exile and as it was to be finally constituted on the day of the Lord, drawing people of all the nations into this eschatological gathering. Each of these assemblies was imaged as an occasion for the word of God to be heard and for a shared meal to be held (see Exod 20:1 and 24:11; Neh 8:1–12; and Isa 2:2–3 and 25:6). For Paul, that image then encountered the existence of the supper clubs and the local associations and called those that were Christian to find the Spirit of God dwelling in their midst, to find the gospel of the crucified and risen Christ converting their usual conversations into a hearing of the word of God, their usual meals into eucharist proclaiming the death of the Lord until he comes, and their usual mutual benevolence into care for God's wretched poor. Their gatherings of the like-minded, thus, were to be turned into *church*, into the assembly of God, a local assembly in communion with the other assemblies. By God's gift, every local assembly around the gospel of Jesus Christ and all the assemblies as a single reality were already the holy convocation of God around the word and the life-giving feast. The existence of this convocation among the Gentiles, including people of all nations, was already a fulfillment of the ancient promise. *Ekklesia* as a name for the gathering belongs thus to Paul's eschatology and to Paul's understanding of the way Scripture creates Christian identity.

Galatians itself gives us evidence that Paul is reusing a scriptural image when he addresses the assemblies. Throughout the letter, like the Gospels after him and on his model, he is calling for reform—for the centrality of the gospel of Jesus Christ; for freedom in Christ; for an end to religious legalism; for mutual correction in a spirit of gentleness; for an end to distinctions between Jew and Greek, slave and free, male and female; and for a faith that is active in love. These things must mark the identity of the assembly of God. The Galatian assemblies are in need of this reform. But where it exists—where what matters is not circumcision or uncircumcision, for example, but the new creation in Christ—then, in his own hand, Paul writes the blessing of peace to those who follow this rule, including them thereby in "the Israel of God" (Gal 6:15–16), the eschatological assembly already present and gathering the nations, the priestly people called together for the sake of witness in the world, as 1 Peter later says (1 Pet 2:9).

As well, Galatians, simply by its use of both the plural and global singular, gives us evidence of the presence of the whole eschatological assembly in each local assembly. The letter to the Corinthians says the matter more clearly, addressed as it is "to the *ekklesia* of God that is in Corinth, to those who are sanctified in Christ Jesus, called to be saints, together with all those who in every place call on the name of our Lord Jesus Christ, both their Lord and ours" (1 Cor 1:2). Local assembly, when it is faithful to the gospel, becomes the way that one is in touch with "those in every place."

In a later style of speech profoundly influenced by this earlier Pauline grammar, the address that begins the account of the death of Polycarp of Smyrna, a beloved second-century martyr and bishop, says the matter more clearly still: "The *ekklesia* of God which sojourns in Smyrna, to the *ekklesia* of God which sojourns in Philomelium, and to all the sojournings of the holy catholic *ekklesia* in every place" (initial inscription). Again, there is a local singular and a global singular; the biblical image applies to both. Each local assembly is entirely church, the presence of the eschatological convocation of God, and a "sojourning" of the holy catholic assembly, to quote those second century Christians of Smyrna. But in Paul's conception, each assembly greets and is greeted by the others, as the "sojourning" at Smyrna greets all the other "sojournings." In Christianity, each place is important, and the very presence of the saving love of God is there, in that locality. Yet each assembly also needs the others. Each assembly should send and receive to and from one another both spiritual gifts and material resources, signs of communion between real places.

It is right then to inquire about "instruments of communion" between the assemblies, like Paul's collection in Macedonia and Achaia for the poor in Jerusalem (Rom 15:25–26; cf. 2 Cor 8–9 and many other places) and like his conception of the blessings of the assembly in Jerusalem in which the Gentile assemblies had come to share (Rom 15:27; cf. 11:17–24). The visits of the apostle and the letters that stood for the apostle and were then to be shared assembly to assembly—as we know from later sources (Col 4:16)—are such instruments. So are the greetings carried by those letters, surrounded as they were with prayers and with ritual acts, like the holy kiss and trinitarian blessings (1 Cor 16:19–24; 2 Cor 13:12–13). So are the passing on and reception in assembly of the more-than-local gospel—including, finally, the four Gospel books themselves—and the signs of Christ in baptism and eucharist, which proclaim and enact that gospel (see 1 Cor 11:23; cf. Rom 6:3–4). And the leadership roles in the church—what we call the ministry—are recognized between the assemblies. Those positions of leadership, in Paul's writing (Rom 12:4–8; 1 Cor 12:27–28), in post-Pauline writing (Eph 4:12), and in the Gospels (Mark 10:44; Matt 24:45–51), have been appointed for the sake of the assembly: for serving, for "building up the body of Christ," for the common good. We have pastors and priests, deacons and bishops, teachers and workers of good for the sake of the assemblies.

Assembly, thus, is the local Christian gathering, in communion with other gatherings, and the local gathering as the dwelling place of the universal gathering, the clearest place to encounter the whole "church." For us, those ancient Hellenistic clubs have long ceased to exist. But the bodily gathering called "the assembly" by Christians has gone on to this day. Perhaps that is so because its identity has been continually reformed to carry the heart of Christian meaning, to become essential to Christianity, the very "body of Christ," as Paul says. In any case, taught by Paul and the Gospels, such reform needs to go on. Our assemblies are by no means perfect but, when they are centered in the gospel and its signs, they are basic to Christianity. "Assembly," then, is not just a local meeting; it is a local meeting in the name and the presence of Jesus Christ, convoked by the Spirit of God, bearing witness to the word and mercy of God present in the world.

Assembly in Theology and Liturgy

Assembly—this biblical name for the local, celebrating Christian community—has had a wide ecumenical currency in our time, with a depth of historical use. We have seen already Ignatius of Antioch "singing the assemblies" on his way to martyrdom. Emeritus has shown his willingness to die for the meeting of Christians, the meeting that gathered in his house around the matter of the risen Lord. Julian of Norwich had that window to the assembly in her cell. We could go on, looking at the early churches as well as at the Middle Ages. At some times, the importance of the communal gathering was clearer than others. But it was always there.

The buildings Christians have built down through the ages, the buildings usually called "churches" in English, have been primarily houses for the assembly. Early on, these involved the conversion of other kinds of buildings for assembly use, beginning at least with the repurposing of the older dwelling then used by an assembly in Dura-Europos, in third-century Syria, but continuing in the fourth and fifth centuries with the conversion of the old Roman public buildings, the basilicas, by making them not only places where a bishop could speak and preside but also and especially places where an assembly could gather around word and sacrament. Sometimes, as the history of Christian architecture unfolded, the assembly was dwarfed by the building. But then with New England meeting houses and African village churches, and even more pointedly with twentieth-century building projects, the importance of the idea of a "house for the assembly" came again to preeminence. Current designs frequently seek to combine into one building a welcome to people—hospitality, ease of movement, the possibility of seeing and hearing—with older accents on the encounter with the holy.

Assembly is, of course, a seriously important word to Lutherans, since already Article VII of the *Augsburg Confession* of 1530 defined the church as "the assembly of all believers among whom the gospel is purely preached and the holy sacraments are administered according to the gospel." Then Luther himself, in his 1539 essay "On the Councils and the Church," in a passage more pastoral and existential than the systematic theological writing of Philip Melanchthon in the *Augsburg Confession*, answered his own question—"how will or how can a poor confused person tell where such Christian holy people are to be found in this world?"—by providing a list of seven quite tangible marks that are all actions in and performed by an assembly: preaching, baptism, the holy supper, absolution, the calling and consecrating of ministers, the public use of thanksgiving and prayer, and the "holy possession of the cross." Even this last mark can be regarded as an assembly-based liturgical practice when it is thought to mean suffering for the gospel, nontriumphalist preaching and prayers, a serving leadership, and a solidarity—in intercessions, collection, and mission—with the sufferings with which the world is so full. For Luther, where one finds these "signs-of-life," one should "not doubt that the true *ecclesia sancta catholica*, 'a Christian holy people' must be, even though their number is very small." It is very clear here that "church" is not an invisible, ideal thing—a "platonic reality" or a "spiritual city"— but a concrete, real gathering of people. From the very beginning of the Lutheran movement, assembly song was an immensely important thing, and cantors saw their task as helping the assembly sing. Hymnals came into existence as important assembly books. In more recent times, the principal document of the Evangelical Lutheran Church in America about the practice of word and sacraments, called *The Use of the Means of Grace*, discusses "Proclamation of the Word and the Christian Assembly," "Baptism and the Christian Assembly," and "Holy Communion and the Christian Assembly," as well as the assembly in mission, as its principal parts.

John Calvin also gives counsel about what should happen in the assembly. In his *Institutes of the Christian Religion*, he argues, drawing from Acts 2:42–47, that any meeting of Christians should always include teaching from the Word, prayer, the Lord's Supper, and almsgiving. This Calvinist weekly practice of the Lord's Supper and that regular inclusion of almsgiving are especially striking and important for us.

"Assembly" is also explicitly present in recent Roman Catholic statements—for example, the 1978 *Environment and Art in Catholic Worship* from the American National Conference of Catholic Bishops, drafted by Robert Hovda: "Among the symbols with which liturgy deals, none is more important than this assembly of believers. . . . The most powerful experience of the sacred is found in the celebration and the persons celebrating, that is, found in the action of the assembly: the living words, the living gestures, the living sacrifice, the living meal." Even more strongly, French Roman Catholic theologian Louis-Marie Chauvet writes, "a church without an *assembly* would be a contradiction in terms. To designate the Christian phenomenon in the process of birth, Christians did not find anything better than applying to it the word 'assembly' or 'church.' This is to say that the gathering . . . is the major characteristic of Christians. From this point of view, Christians are people who join their sisters and brothers in an assembly in the name and memory of Jesus. Such an assembly is the Christians' *primary mark* or . . . the 'fundamental sacrament' of the risen Christ."

"Assembly" appears in Anglican circles as well. For one thing, the basic book of the Anglican churches is named *The Book of Common Prayer*, where "common" means exactly *not private* (and certainly not *ordinary*) but *shared* or *together*—and thus *in assembly*. Although the principal terms used in Church of England essays encouraging the "parish communion" in the 1930s were "the local congregation" and "the parish," on the very first page of Gabriel Hebert's important introductory essay in the volume *The Parish Communion*, this sentence appears: "By 'the Parish Communion' is meant the celebration of the Holy Eucharist, with the communion of the people, in a parish church, as the chief service of the day, or, better, as the assembly of the Christian community for the worship of God." Moreover, current Anglican liturgical scholarship also readily speaks of "the assembly" when it wants to discuss healthy contemporary practice and meaning. Similar usage can be found among the Orthodox, Old Catholics, Methodists, Pentecostals, and the Reformed. And Presbyterians make use of a *Book of Common Worship*.

So most of us Christians, of whatever communion, have in diverse ways had *assemblies* in which we participate in the mysteries of Christ, forming us to find faith again and so to care about our neighbors and all the world. We have assemblies centered on and actively engaged in the word and sacraments of Jesus Christ, the word and the sacraments that are meant for communities, meant to "make the church." We need to note this stunning ecumenical fact even though the ways of connecting and governing the assemblies differ among us: whatever else may be said about our divisions, we do begin to recognize in the other communities something that looks like church when we see those assemblies.

The liturgical movement of the twentieth century encouraged the recovery of the importance of assembly. Assembly song was back and musicians were once again "leaders of assembly song." Instead of calling the minister leading the Christian meeting the "celebrant," Christian liturgists in many churches urged the use of the old term *presider*, the term already present in the *First Apology* of Justin Martyr in the second century. The whole assembly celebrates. Our bishop, priest, or pastor presides in our midst. Against both individualism and crowd mentality, some teachers began to talk of the "personal-communal experience" as belonging to healthy liturgy. Support for such a communal experience called for simplicity, accessibility, capacity for bearing mystery, and a sense of service in the words, gestures, art, and music used in liturgy. Robert Hovda rightly wrote that this "rules out anything trivial and self-centered, anything fake, cheap or shoddy, anything pretentious or superficial." Such quality enables both a deep respect for each person and the constituting of a centered community around the basic symbols of the faith.

So in the Bible and in ecumenical liturgy, *assembly* matters. It is Paul's biblical name for the gathering of Christians. It is everywhere in the New Testament. With Chauvet, it is an essential characteristic of Christians and the Christians' primary sign of the risen Christ. But however we would say it, this much is true: together we have treasured the assembly and have aimed for its ongoing renewal. Such renewal always includes an awareness that baptism forms us into a community; that in such communities, accent must always be placed on the dignity and equality of all the baptized; that full participation in the holy things of God's gift forms the center of this communal life; and that this assembly is always being turned toward a needy world in service, witness, and love.

Learning Assembly by Heart

This historic, essential assembly is still among us. But its continued existence and well-being call for us to learn its contours and its practice by heart. We need to treasure it. We need to know in our bones that being Christian is a communal undertaking. We need to honor the other members of whatever assembly is ours, the diverse members of the body of Christ, even if we do not necessarily personally "like" them. In Christianity, we do not just "go to church"; we gather with an assembly.

And then we are made church. We "do church." Or church happens, as a communal event. For the assembly is not simply a meeting. It is a meeting with a very specific content. We also need to know that content by heart—the central matters of our gathering, the shape and flow of what we do together, our public common work, our liturgy. Sunday after Sunday, the fourfold Gathering, Word, Meal, and Sending shape us as assembly. We need our principal leader to preside among us, and we need our musicians primarily to lead assembly song.

All of the characteristics of assembly that we have seen in the Bible and theology call for our practice. With Paul, we will know that the assembly needs to be continually reformed to center on the gospel of Jesus Christ and to welcome all so as to be indeed a sign of the convocation of God for all peoples and to be a participation already now in that convocation. With Paul, we will know that the assemblies are to greet one another and share central signs of communion with one another, and so we will treasure the ecumenical liturgical shape and the ecumenical lectionary and the presiding ministers who come to us, commended to us by at least part of the whole church. With Paul and the Gospels, we will call upon all our leaders to see themselves as servants of the assembly and its purpose in Jesus Christ. We will also need to treasure the larger forms of assembly with which our assembly is a means of communion: our diocese or synod and its bishop, our national church, our commitment to the ecumenical movement. With the Gospels, we will know that the amazing gift of God to our assembly is the presence of the risen Christ in our midst and the Spirit poured out from him, the very Spirit that enlivens our meeting.

With Mark, we will meet in our houses for the assembly, and we will welcome Christ in the presence of the least ones. With Matthew, we will teach and baptize and practice reconciliation. With Luke, we will seek to speak of Christ in all the Scriptures, and we will share the bread. With John, we will meet on Sunday, and we will treasure the Gospel books. With the author of 1 Peter, we will find ourselves—we who are "no people"—being made into God's people, with a call to bear witness to God's mercy for the life of the world. And listening to the elder John who saw the Revelation, we will let ourselves be exhorted toward healthier assembly life and witness.

Then with the ancient Christians of Smyrna, we will know that we are sojourning as the people of God in a very specific place. Indeed, with the Jerusalem community in Acts 2 and with Justin's assembly in second-century Rome, we too will gather together in one place. We need to learn again and again to honor and love that place, bearing witness to God and serving our neighbors exactly there. With the Christians of Dura and of the fourth-century Christian basilicas, we will ask if our buildings house the assembly and give it a center. If not, we will seek to reform them. With Luther, we will need to care about the clear presence of all the marks of the church, the "signs of life" that make our assembly recognizable as the holy people of God, available to any "poor person" looking for church. With Calvin, we will restore the Word, Prayers, Meal, and Almsgiving. With Jean-Marie Chauvet, we will treasure this truth: assembly—our assembly, if it is faithful and whether or not it is ideal—is the basic mark of Christians and the fundamental sacrament of the risen Christ. With Dietrich Bonhoeffer, we will know that when we gather there, we come to encounter Jesus Christ and become part of Jesus Christ existing as assembly. And we will hope that, with Emeritus, we will even be willing to die for the assembly.

In the Lord's Prayer, Christians have especially prayed that the forgiveness of the end times and the bread of God's final feast will already be present among us—among *us*, in our mutual forgiveness and in our own common Meal. The plural *we* and *our* of the Lord's Prayer are first of all about the assembly. Because of Jesus Christ, forgiveness and bread are there, forming us to turn to our needy world. We need that assembly, that biblical and liturgical reality, again and again.

Such knowing by heart belongs to the spirituality of assembly.

* * *

When I was first becoming a pastor, I was given the charge of a very small campus assembly at a university in the southern United States. One Sunday, as I was presiding behind the table, facing the small assembly across the table, a little girl stepped out of the pews into the central aisle, in the middle of the church building and directly opposite me. She slowly raised her hands, mimicking the way my hands were raised, and we finished the thanksgiving prayer that way, together. I will never forget that girl. We—and all those around us—were church together.

The posture both she and I were using is called orans, *"praying." It is the posture in which entire assemblies of ancient Christians stood as they gave thanks and prayed. It can be seen everywhere in the wall paintings of the Christian catacombs of Rome. With open hands and graciously bent and upraised arms, the person praying stands in a form like a cup, open to God and the universe. It is nearly universally recognizable as a posture for praise and prayer. And it is much like the slightly more modest posture of open hands with which Muslims pray. The liturgical movement has recovered it, at least for presiders praying at the eucharistic table. But here and there, some assemblies have realized that it used to belong to the whole assembly, and they have recovered it for everyone. You may have seen it or participated in it in Pentecostal or Evangelical churches. I also knew its full-assembly use in the Philadelphia Episcopal Cathedral, where when the eucharist was celebrated, everyone stood in a great circle around the table, arms upraised.*

One of my favorite images of a person in orans *can be found in a small subterranean chamber in the Catacombs of Priscilla in Rome. There, a woman—she is called the* Velata, *the "veiled woman," because she has a long cloth over her head, and we do not know her name—stands imaged as praying. She is doubtless the woman whose body was originally placed in this chamber. Behind her we see what is likely an image of her wedding and an image of her caring for her child. Some commentators have thought the image of her praying means to* let us see what she looks like in paradise now that she is dead. But no matter what the original intention of the painting, I think she looks like she did in the assembly, when she was praying with the community. Around the chamber, on walls and ceiling, are yet other images, all images of salvation: Christ carrying a lamb, Noah surviving the flood, Jonah coming out of the great fish, Isaac being spared, and the three Jews surviving Nebuchadnezzar's furnace. Noah and the three Jews are especially fascinating because they too stand in orans *as if* they are joining the veiled woman in prayer in the assembly. In each of these cases, an image like a great bird descends upon the figure—Noah's dove, perhaps, and the presence of the "one like a son of God" who is in the fire with the three Jews. Jonah's arms, as he comes out of the fish, here also extend in prayer.

All of that was there for me when the girl stood in the midst of the church and raised her hands. I was not alone. We were church together. And though no one else raised their hands, the axis between her and me pulled all the others in. My ministry and the ministry of the girl were for the sake of the assembly. Around the holy table, in the act of thanksgiving, we were assembly together. And we were assembly with the veiled woman and Noah, Jonah, and the three Jews surviving. So it continues. We too, in assembly, have the Spirit poured out on us and the risen Christ standing with us, promising life.

2

Why Is the Assembly Important?

Perhaps the meeting continues like this: A single person rises and goes to the reading desk, where the large book that was carried in the entrance procession has been placed. With measured but lively voice, this person reads an appointed passage from the Old Testament so that all can hear, ending with the acclamation, "Word of God, word of life!" The assembly responds, "Thanks be to God," and the reader is seated. Then a cantor begins to lead the assembly in singing a psalm in response to the reading. A brief silence ensues, as if the words that have been read and then sung are too important not to let them simply echo for a while in the room and in the hearts of the hearers. The reader then rises again, this time to read a passage from the first-century letters of Paul. Again, the same acclamation and the same brief silence follow. The cantor, this time joined by a choir, leads the assembly in singing multiple Alleluias entwined with a verse addressed to Christ, as if to welcome the risen One in the Gospel text that is about to be proclaimed. During this singing, the assembly rises and the book is carried into the midst of the room, surrounded by candles. The presider follows the book and the candles and, still in the midst, reads a text from one of the four Gospels. The assembly speaks acclamations of praise around this reading, as if continuing to address Christ, present in the very words. The book is then carried back to the reading desk, and the assembly is seated. The presider, who has followed the book to the reading desk, now preaches from that place, using the images with which the texts of the day are full to articulate the world's need for God's grace and to give that grace freely by verbally wrapping the hearers in the promise and presence of the triune God. Once again, a silence ensues. Out of that silence, the assembly rises and sings a vigorous hymn, one that also uses and adds to the images in the texts. Then as a response to the words that have been heard and sung, a response arising from trust in those promises, yet another assisting minister comes to the same reading desk to lead the assembly in a series of intercessions—articulating before God the actual and pressing needs of the church, the world, and the assembly's locality—with the assembly responding aloud to each of these bids in a short prayerful acclamation. Finally, as if to seal these prayers by a mutual sign of communal reconciliation, the presider bids the members of the assembly to greet those immediately around them in peace, and they do so, each one being a sign of the risen Christ to the other.

Such may be "the Word," the second part of the ecumenical fourfold order in the Sunday meeting of an assembly. At least such might be one way the Word is celebrated by a particular assembly. There certainly are other ways, other styles of communal practice, though they will all include an assembly listening to the Scriptures read, hearing their meanings proclaimed, and responding in song and prayer.

This part of the meeting explicitly involves *meaning*: scriptural images and narratives to hold and interpret our experience, text next to text next to text, each influencing how we read the others; a whole universe of juxtaposed meanings that individuals as well as the entire community may use to rediscover their own identities; the texts all together next to one person preaching in the hearing of all and that combination yielding hope and trust in God; that trust expressed in song and especially in intercessions for the great needs of the world; and each member of the assembly speaking peace to some of the others. Then this word-and-meaning event is juxtaposed with the eucharist and with the communal sending, spinning out the significance of the meeting yet further. That whole complex enacts the way Christians read the Bible and is manifestly intended to bring Christian meanings to expression.

It is appropriate for us to ask about those meanings. What are they? Can we rightly say that such meanings are important to life in our time? And if the assembly itself is an expression of those meanings, can we then articulate why that assembly is so important? Giving some answer to those questions will belong to a spirituality of the assembly and will assist us further in learning the assembly by heart.

The first and most important answer, of course, arises from what we have already said about the New Testament understandings of "church" and their liturgical elaboration. We have seen that *assembling together* is the primary biblical and liturgical understanding of church: whatever "salvation" is, we are saved together, not alone. That assertion can surprise us. Many nineteenth-century conceptions of Christianity—conceptions still quite alive today—understood the meaning of Christianity as fulfilled in helping individuals "go to heaven." But it is difficult to find such ideas in the Bible itself, and they are almost totally absent from the historic Christian liturgy. Rather, as 1 Peter has it, we "no people" are being made "a people together" in order thus to find our identity graciously given to us and in order to bear witness in this world to the mercy of God. Or, as Paul has it in Galatians, we are being called together to trust in this God and being set free together—as "the Israel of God"—to exercise that trust in active love toward our neighbors. As Dietrich Bonhoeffer has it, church is Christ existing now as assembly. And as Louis-Marie Chauvet says it, assembly is the primary sacrament of the risen Christ. Such ideas matter a great deal in a world where people long for identity but where individualism—"me first"—seems to reign. In the trust that such a biblical and liturgical understanding does matter for the contemporary world, this reality of assembly should be present and practiced among us. This first answer thus involves the biblical and liturgical understanding that assembly is integral to Christianity and that assembly, when it is faithful to this image, calls us all again and again to faith and to faith active in love. That is why assembly is important. With Emeritus, we Christians cannot live without it.

But there is more to say. That biblical understanding itself and its gifts to our times should be explored more fully. We may articulate the importance of assembly by doing so not only in biblical ways, as alive in the liturgy, but also in exploring how such a biblical and liturgical understanding responds to current social and human needs. Such a response includes at least these things: rituals and symbols that interpret our world and our lives and are shared with others, communities that awaken in us trust and compassion, and the availability of a steady experience of material reality. Let us seek to articulate each of these as a way to express the importance of assembly to our own times.

We Need Shared Ritual and Symbol

The assembly, together with its reliable ritual repetitions, is a large part of the answer Christians may give to the current, aching need for a helpful public symbolism. Are there symbols that can both help individuals discover meaning and, at the same time, orient the individual toward the common good? Can we share those symbols? Many people in the present time fear that we cannot; they think we have lost shared ways of organizing a meaningful world. Or, to say the matter in another way, society has been in these decades challenged to find a public set of symbols capable of holding us in material and social realities, giving new grounds for hope and a social context for the functioning of the individual mind.

Suzanne Langer, a mid-twentieth-century American philosopher who especially articulated the challenge in this latter way, did not think that such a public symbolism would come from the churches. For her, the churches were too devoted to the petty and the ugly. One should grant that this judgment may often be true. But local Christian assemblies have worked to prove her wrong. The model gathering with which this chapter began—the gathering around the manifold images of the Scriptures, images that then are turned to embrace meanings both for individual lives and for the honestly expressed needs of the whole world—is already a "public symbolism." The intercessions in the Sunday meeting, when they are carefully and responsibly crafted, demonstrate a specific exercise of such symbolism. But so does the Meal that follows, with its thanksgiving and its communal sharing of food in such a way that there is always some—even though only a fragment—for everyone. So also does the climax of the total event in a Sending that turns each of the participants and the whole group toward the surrounding world with a call to exercise what has been seen and heard in the meeting—individuals united with care for societal well-being and food and help for the hungry.

The primary symbol enacted in this meeting, as we have seen, is the assembly itself as a symbol for the risen Christ. If that is so, then when we come to the meeting, we are able to see again who Christ is. The body of Christ, we discover again and again, is composed of a rich variety of people. The risen Christ embraces each one of us but is also always other than the isolated self, than "me" alone. As the nineteenth-century Jesuit poet Gerard Manley Hopkins put it,

> Christ plays in ten thousand places,
> Lovely in limbs, and lovely in eyes not his
> To the Father through the features of men's faces.

We may see that play in the assembly. I encounter Jesus Christ in those somewhat like me but also and especially in those seemingly unlike me: in the other-abled man in a wheelchair who greets me as an usher at the door, in the gay man presiding, in the older woman of European origin reading, in the cantor of African origin singing, in the transgender crucifer leading the procession, in the teenagers holding candles around the Gospel reading, in the older man of Latin origin leading the intercessions, in the child greeting me with the peace of the Lord, in the middle-aged man of Asian origin ministering the Cup of the supper to me, and in all of them together praying and singing. All of those diversities may not be present in any one assembly, but some of them surely are, and the trajectory of life in Christ is always toward broader inclusion. Baptism joins us to the assembly, and the baptismal assertion of Paul continues to press our assemblies: "As many of you as were baptized into Christ have clothed yourselves with Christ. There is no longer Jew or Greek, there is no longer slave or free, there is no longer male and female; for all of you are one in Christ Jesus" (Gal 3:27–28).

In any case, despite seeming social similarities, the other is not me. In encountering *not me*, my understanding of God and of the world is continually challenged to grow and change. By those limbs and eyes around me, by Jesus Christ existing as assembly, I am called to greater empathy and compassion. Then with the whole assembly, I am sent to make signs of that empathy and compassion in the world. Seen in this way—practiced in this way—the assembly itself is a public symbol.

But there is more. The assembly practices a variety of specific symbols that have a strong resonance with daily life. Gathering around a water pool (and sometimes using it to bathe those who join the assembly), reading from that great Book, celebrating that Meal focused on a common loaf of bread and a shared cup of wine, singing together: these all are what Albert Borgmann and Richard Gaillardetz have called "focal practices." They engage a community in a quite ordinary activity—washing, listening to a story, eating, singing—with the good that is sought in that activity and internal to the practice itself, such as cleanness, immersion in a narrative or a poem, nourishment, or a sense of harmony. They require attention from the group and certain skills. And though ordinary, they can be quite beautiful. We recognize the Bath, the Book, the Meal, the Song as matters that might be found in daily life—and *are* sometimes found in daily life—though in the assembly, they are heightened and more clear. They are made somehow larger. Indeed, their clear practice in the assembly can sometimes feel like a countercultural undertaking in a time when quick showers have replaced baths, families seldom gather around an evening reading of a book, people often do not eat together and festal meals are rare, and most people no longer sing.

Furthermore, in the assembly, these practices have slightly shifted: even if the person being washed is an adult, the community and its presider are responsible to do the washing. A large group is listening to this book being read; a large group is eating this meal, a meal practiced like the most remarkable banquet but with only fragments of food received. And the singing is intentionally for everyone, though sometimes lead by a choir, a group of rehearsed voices. Still, we recognize these practices and see that they have symbolic resonance with daily life. We know that Christianity has used these very common yet deeply meaningful practices, these basic human things, to bear its central meanings: this Bath is a washing into Christ, this Book is the word of God, this Meal is the body and blood of Christ given "for you," this Singing is the church enacting its unity in the Spirit.

Of course, just as we have sometimes shrunk focal practices to become easily obtained commodities in our daily societal life, that same shrinking has also afflicted the churches. The Bath can become a sprinkling. The Book can be replaced by a few words projected on a screen. The Meal can become a prepackaged sip of juice and a wafer. The Song can be recorded. And the assembly can be made simply into observers of these things being used, not attentive participants in the focal undertaking. Communal skill and attention can be dissipated. But where this shrinking and dissipation have been resisted, where the symbols have been made larger and are communally enacted, the assembly does indeed practice a public symbolism with public meaning for the world.

Take the Book as example. An assembly gathers around a book—a Bible, a lectionary, or a Gospel book—at its center, like a large family gathering to hear a story read or like a court anchoring the reliability of its proceedings in oaths sworn on the great book. The Book and assembly go together: without the Book, the assembly has no center; without the assembly, the Book is crippled in purpose. The very fact of the Book then makes clear the permanence of these words and symbolizes such scriptural sayings as "the word of our God will stand forever" (Isa 40:8). Still, the assembly is not a print event but a living event of human voices, now. And that central book requires interpreting, not least because it comes from a different time than ours and because all of its parts do not say the same thing. The book is not a single ideology but an embracing and various library. So in the assembly, the Bible—*ta biblia*, "the books," in Greek—becomes the ground from which fresh words are elaborated, spoken into the present moment in preaching, in intercessions, and in hymn choices. Live human voices, echoing in the assembly's room, make the written words present in a communally accessible way. The old words are made to interpret the present world and to speak of God's mercy in Christ to that world.

The very fact of the Book also makes clear that whatever is read in the assembly is part of a larger whole, a dialogue between a great variety of voices. For Christians, the organizing center of that whole is the crucified and risen Christ present to the assembly in the readings. Any Gospel reading is part of the whole Gospel book, leaning forward to the account of Jesus's death, resurrection, and appearance in the assemblies. The very fact of the Book also includes the spaces between its constituent books and between its chapters and verses. The meanings of the Book include these silences, these tensions between parts, sometimes echoed by the silences in the assembly and always echoed by the constant use in the meeting of more than one passage of Scripture.

Such a practice with the Book enacts a public symbolism. The meanings elaborated in the assembly are meanings for individuals but also for the life of the world. And the focal practice of reading and speaking from the Book, renewed again and again in the assembly, can be restored elsewhere—as the family or other people who live together once again may read a book together or as the Bible may be read at home in a rebirth of "domestic church."

Much the same may be said of the Bath and Meal and Song. They too are public symbols. They too, practiced in the communal gathering, have meanings for individuals and for the life of the world. They too invite us to a larger personal practice: to remembering baptism daily; to learning to sing again at home; and especially to practicing shared, focused, and hospitable meals in our homes.

But there is yet more. The public symbolism of the assembly also includes bodily gestures and metaphoric language. The bodies of those in the assembly matter. All of our senses engage with the assembly events. All our bodies become, as it were, one body. And we sometimes indicate that with gestures. As we are able—and representing those who are not able—we stand together, recalling that the resurrection of Christ has raised us up and made us stand upon the reliability of God's mercy (see 1 Cor 15:1 and 16:13). We all put out our hands, like beggars in a food line, for that mercy in the Bread and Cup of the holy Meal. We make gestures of peace—a handshake or, more profoundly and graciously, perhaps, the holding of one another's forearms or a deep bow. We may learn to raise our arms in prayer in the *orans* posture, echoing our presider in the great thanksgiving of the eucharist. Doing this together, we are individuals—embodied *persons*—but persons in assembly, and the gestures we make may counterculturally suggest to our surrounding world that bodies matter.

Words also matter. In a literalistic culture, the metaphors with which Christian assembly practice can be full, especially when these metaphors are renewed by drawing from the sources of biblical rhetoric, do propose a richer way of thinking. Literalism flattens language, easily turning religious speech into a weapon against others who do not agree. At its best, assembly practice works instead with biblical metaphors, with those expressions that name something accurately by using the wrong word. Our God is a rock, a castle, a fountain, a fire, a shepherd, and astoundingly, a lamb. There is more room for many people, for a diverse community, to meet together as one in such metaphors than there is in a literalistic assertion. This language use also evidences the practice of a public symbolism to hold and orient us in material and social realities. At its best, the Christian assembly does not offer explanations but images to hold and orient our life in the world.

At its best. Our assemblies are by no means always at their best. These ritual and symbolic practices need continual renewal among us. A given assembly may usually be almost entirely seated, with gestures unwelcome. The intercessions may not be responsibly crafted, paying attention to both the promises of God and the real needs of the world, but functioning as exercises in focusing only on ourselves. The food of the eucharist may not be recognizable as food. The hymns may be randomly chosen, the Scripture absent or read so that it cannot be heard or understood. The primary symbols may have been allowed to shrink to religious commodities we "get" rather than focal practices that engage us all. Our assembly may not have worked on welcoming the other, may even have let itself become a closed society of the like-minded, in spite of what Paul says. Still, renewal and recovery go on. Learning the assembly by heart—learning that healthy assembly is a needed and shared practice of public symbolism—can help reinvigorate that renewal.

We Need Communities of Trust and Compassion

Our hope for renewed assemblies, a hope reawakened during the coronavirus pandemic when such assemblies were for a while and for good reason lost to us, can be seen as part of a current movement toward increased communal engagement. Robert Putnam, the very author who in *Bowling Alone* pointed to widespread communal disengagement of which the decline in mainline church attendance was one manifestation, has—together with Shaylyn Romney Garrett—engagingly written of "the upswing" in a book by that title. This upswing, they say, involves a possible social turn from a long period where the *I* had primary accent to a time with a renewed accent on *we*. These authors look at the emergence now of engaged communities that are not just created by familial or workplace bonds, that are local and participatory, and that have an aim or purpose that is more than simply being together. Religious institutions were included in their purview, though they looked much more broadly. After a long period of decline, the authors hope such communities are coming into existence again and will contribute to the further emergence of greater equality in economics, more compromise in politics, greater cohesion in society, and more altruism in culture. Putnam and Garrett thus were looking for groups marked by "bridging" (the crossing of usual social boundaries) rather than simply "bonding" (the linking of the like-minded or the socially similar). These authors hope that such groups marked by bridging can also be workshops for building trust between people and for encouraging compassion.

The Christian assembly we have been describing fits many of these interests, especially if it has been working on an open door to diversity and on the practice of public symbolism. Such an assembly is indeed a local, participatory, more-than-familial group with a greater purpose than simply being together. Christians should rejoice in evidence of a social movement from *I* to *we*, should willingly see their own congregations as part of that movement, and should certainly be glad, in these divided times, for greater economic parity, political compromise, social cohesion, altruism, and mutual trust. The assembly we have been considering is a social unit, part of our actual society, and this sociological analysis of the needs of our current time does help us see why assembly—or *renewed* assembly—is so important.

Still, there is more to say. Christian assemblies have by no means always been places that have encouraged the growth of mutual trust, political compromise, and social cohesion. The recent history of sexual abuse by clergy represents a shameful example of our failure. So do those congregations that recently insisted upon meeting in person when such meeting would almost certainly lead to the neighborhood spread of the coronavirus, especially when such insistence was accompanied by the argument that the virus was itself politically motivated "fake news." Many pastors can report long histories of fierce arguments and even schisms in local congregations, sometimes over relatively minor matters, such as times for Sunday services or whether to repave the parking lot.

Still, at its best, a Christian assembly should understand that its center is not in political agreement but in the central symbols that proclaim and enable our participation in the mercy of the triune God. Its unity is in Christ. And that center makes possible the mutual gathering of a wide variety of people with a wide variety of opinions, a social cohesion that does not rest on uniformity or like-mindedness. That center should enable "bridging" even more than "bonding." That center in Christ invites us all to avoid the false dreams of direct access to the other or power over the other, dreams that in their erotic form do lead to abuse. As we have said, we encounter one another much more profoundly and freely through our shared symbols. But then such a personal communal assembly—such a centered yet open assembly—does contribute to realized possibilities for social cohesion and compromise, for openness to diverse opinions and to empathy. It is Christ who matters; our own opinions are decidedly secondary. In Christ, we can forgive one another, and compromise on secondary matters should always be possible. Reasonable and honest discussion ought to be available to us. In any case, Jesus Christ always turns us toward the stranger and the other, the wretched and the poor; the assembly is sent to care for the neighbor in incidents of altruism.

Of course, such hopes depend on the continued renewal of the assembly and the strong and continually restored central presence of the symbols that matter for assembly identity. Moreover, honesty compels us to admit that assemblies in the foreseeable future may be fewer and smaller, not least because the extended time of absence from assembly during the pandemic may have changed the habits of many people. Such decrease in size must not discourage us. The mustard seed—indeed, the mustard bush!—is tiny in the Gospel parable, yet it welcomes the birds of the air. The seed falls into the earth and dies, yet it yields hundredfold. And the cross, that death to which both of these images were meant to point, is nothing in the history of the power of nations, yet it draws all to itself. Those old Christian images still matter. Against an ideology of growth and size, a dream that we must always be larger, these images encourage a contrary way. But smallness must also not bewitch us into focusing only on ourselves. The "people of God," however few, exist to be priests for the whole world; they bear witness for the life of the world. The idea of being the "elect," the chosen of God, can be disastrously misunderstood without remembering that vocation.

So let the assembly be stable and serious in its purpose to be centered on the gospel of Jesus Christ, gathered by the Sprit into the life of the holy Trinity, and sent again and again to give signs of love in the world. But let it be open and permeable to anyone who would come to see what it is doing and anyone who might then be drawn to join in that purpose. Let the people love the place in the world where their assembly lives and serves, yet let them know that assembly's connection to the wider world: the whole church in all the world and the whole world to which that church bears witness. Let any assembly know that it is a microcosm of that larger church and yet, at the same time, an important local unit in ecumenical unity.

In those ways, the assembly, however small or large, will indeed be a place for the incubation of social cohesion, human unity, healthy compromise, compassion, and trust.

We Need a Steady Experience of Material Reality

After the experience of isolation during the pandemic, an assembly of real people—in the flesh, seeing each other, breathing together, enacting the central Christian symbols in common—will have been for us a sudden gift. We have come out of that necessary isolation deeply grateful for the technological means that enabled us to stay at least somewhat connected with others. But we also need to be aware of the dangers of that technology, carefully considering how to use such means as tools that do not overwhelm us or take over our lives. Furthermore, the importance of focal practices to the Christian assembly, the Book and Meal and Song we have considered here, and the history of wise counsel against using pretense or anything artificial in Christian liturgy both point out the assembly as a place for encounter with material reality. Our need for such encounters is one of the reasons the assembly is so important. A spirituality of the assembly calls for us to think about that need a little more profoundly.

Consider, for example, the comparison between liturgy and drama. Many people have noted similarities between a communal liturgy and a staged play. For one thing, both are scripted or largely scripted. Both usually involve many actors. Both are concerned with communication and have moments of intensity and emotional resolution. But then the similarity ceases. In liturgy, the script—the *ordo* together with the texts of the liturgy—is openly known, not hidden. The liturgy belongs to us all. Indeed, in liturgy, at least ideally, there is no audience; all are encouraged to participate actively. And most importantly, in liturgy, we are not pretending: we are who we really are and we are that together, before God. What we do we do as ourselves in this world. We are in earnest. We are not acting as if we are someone else, nor are we pretending that the conclusion of the play is unknown, using the illusion of spontaneity and surprise. Such illusions, in drama as also in written fiction, can be quite important, causing us to see something new about the world or bringing us to experience pity and sorrow, or delight and joy.

But for all of the fictive character of some of the images of the Scripture, fiction is not how liturgy works. It may be that someone attending a performance of, say, *Hamlet* for the tenth time, someone who has committed large parts of the script to memory, will experience the play a little like experiencing a liturgy. But that playgoer will still be in the audience, not on the stage, and will know that the characters in the play are not actually the same as the personal identity of the actors. It may also be that some leaders in liturgy do their ritual work for the community as if they are actors taking on a role. But congregations readily recognize insincerity and pretense. For healthy liturgy, reality—being who we actually are, praying about what we actually experience, hoping for our real and material world—is of foundational significance.

That reality—that absence of pretense—is important in yet other ways. While the technology of musical recording has gotten better and better at reproducing sound, wise musical leadership in the church urges us not to use recorded music in communal liturgy. Music in the liturgy requires the actual breath and the actual sense of time of the gathered bodies. Singing with a previously recorded accompaniment lacks life and breath. Singing with whatever talent is actually in the room feels quite alive, even if it is not a brilliant performance. Singing together with a musician and a choir who, like us and at the same time, are bringing their own faith to expression and seeking to praise God with us makes it clear that the musicians are also part of the assembly.

More, the liturgical renewal movement of our time has brought us to see that the physical things of liturgical use—candlelight and fire, bread and wine, books and clothing—ought not be replaced by substitutes, such as artificial candles, pretend fire, wafer bread that is difficult to recognize as bread, individual plastic containers of a little bread and grape juice, and so on. Rather, a goal in our time is to try to make our assemblies places of larger not shrunken symbols, places of encounter with what is materially real. It is better to use books rather than throwaway sheets of paper, for example; better to use loaves of bread, leavened or unleavened, that we then share together. The deep sense of the liturgy is resistant to pretense.

But then we come to the question that urgently presented itself during the time of the pandemic and now continues: What about participation in liturgy through recorded or livestreamed digital means? When churches, for good reason, were not able to meet, many creative alternatives were found. Indeed, pastors and congregational leaders were for a while regularly reporting that participation in online sources—in livestreamed, Zoom-shared, and recorded liturgies—was higher in number than average attendance before the pandemic began. Then electronic weariness set in, and researchers began to find far lower participation numbers than had been the case before the pandemic. Still, such videotaping or livestreaming will likely continue. There are indeed people who will continue to need this distanced connection to a congregation, people for whom this access is a new and now beloved gift, making some kind of connection possible when illness or difficulty in movement would otherwise exclude them. But there are also people who simply want to be able to surf through a variety of digital offerings in a sort of new church-shopping that does not require commitment. Moreover, there have been a number of experiments with celebrating eucharist, with people at home setting their own bread and wine before the computer screen and then consuming it. What can we make of these practices? Is this the assembly about which we have been thinking?

Consider this: Francis, the Bishop of Rome, has recently called for a reemergence of dialogue and empathy in human life. In doing so, he also warned about the misuse of computer-based communication: "We fed ourselves on dreams of splendor and grandeur, and ended up consuming distraction, insularity and solitude. We gorged ourselves on networking, and lost the taste of fraternity.... Prisoners of a virtual reality, we lost the taste and flavor of the truly real." Part of Francis's concern was the ease with which digital media can be used to speak ill of others or to decide quickly what we like and do not like, isolating us from a wider world. He continued,

> Digital media can also expose people to the risk of addiction, isolation and a gradual loss of contact with concrete reality, blocking the development of authentic interpersonal relationships. They lack the physical gestures, facial expressions, moments of silence, body language and even the smells, the trembling of hands, the blushes and perspiration that speak to us and are a part of human communication. Digital relationships, which do not demand the slow and gradual cultivation of friendships, stable interaction or the building of a consensus that matures over time, have the appearance of sociability. Yet they do not really build community; instead, they tend to disguise and expand the very individualism that finds expression in xenophobia and in contempt for the vulnerable. Digital connectivity is not enough to build bridges. It is not capable of uniting humanity.... True wisdom demands an encounter with reality.

One way to underline what Francis has written would include an awareness of what many thinkers about the effects of the internet on human consciousness are saying: steady computer use with steady internet access erodes our attention. Francis calls this "distraction." Healthy Christian liturgy necessarily involves attention: attention to one another, attention to the focal practices, attention to the Scripture, attention to God, and attention to the neighbor and the world.

While Francis is not writing about digital media used for liturgy, his warning is still important. His call for attention to "physical gestures, facial expressions, moments of silence, body language and even the smells" does belong to our sense that a healthy assembly presents us with a steady experience of material reality and the presence of living persons, and we need that experience.

Of course, *reality* and *the real* are words that give us significant difficulties. Long philosophical debates have pursued the question "What is real?" And our popular English usage does not always help us. For example, when we speak of "reality television," we mean shows that purportedly document actual life situations. Everything depends on that word *purportedly*! Besides often feeling abusive, these shows frequently feel like another case of a scripted drama where the script is hidden. But Christian use of the word *real* arises from faith in a God incarnate and known in the flesh, sanctifying the presence of human persons, the very material of existence, and all the stuff of the cosmos. This presence and materiality belong to Christian assembly.

So let it be said clearly: these electronic means we have used have involved memories of assembly, sometimes quite beautiful memories, but not the assembly itself, that classic reality essential to Christianity. We do need to be grateful for the tools that have enabled many of us to stay in touch with one another in this time. Some of those tools have been remarkably helpful in supporting prayer and spirituality. In regard to assembling together during the time when assembly was dangerous to communal health, especially to the health of the vulnerable, we mostly did as well as we could with what we had. There should be peaceful thanksgiving about what was possible. But absent the actual presence of human beings to one another and absent their use of material stuff, we did not hold the assembly. It is important that we acknowledge that. And then we should gladly continue to recover the assembly itself.

In making this assertion about the absence of assembly in electronic representation, one might again consider the various reasons that support this argument but also help illumine what assembly actually is:

- The assembly in Bible and liturgy "sojourns" in a real local place, witnesses to God's love for a real place. The electronic replacement for place, when it is used as a liturgical gathering tool, comes too close to using pretense in worship. For the sake of telling the truth about the mystery of God and the world, that pretense must be avoided. Christians need to resist the technological recasting of what we think is real. A religion that rejoices that God has come among us in the flesh must not support the idea that pixels on a screen are just as real or even more real than an actual place, nor that the digital "ether" is more spiritual than human beings being together bodily.
- "To be," the pre-Socratic Greek philosopher Archytas rightly said, "is to be in some place." The assembly occurs, *is*, *takes place*.
- The assembly is not simply a meeting, which might indeed be electronic, using digital tools to enable communication and discussion, but a centered meeting, a meeting around Christ in word and sacrament. The identity of the meeting is transformed by that center like the Christian versions of the old *collegia* were transformed to be the assembly of God, as witnessed in the New Testament.
- We certainly can read the Scripture at home. Perhaps we can read a sermon or listen to or watch a recorded sermon. We can also pray, and it may be that Zoom is a helpful tool for several people praying together. But the assembly is *word next to sacrament* leading us again to faith and turning us toward our neighbor's need. That juxtaposition we cannot enact at home by ourselves.
- We do not baptize ourselves; baptism always requires at least one other person, the baptizer. The word of

absolution needs to be a living voice in our ears; it cannot be recorded. As well (and as we shall consider in the next chapter), eucharist is an event that happens to an assembly, not a commodity confected by a "celebrant." More, laying on of hands is a profound sign of prayer for another, used in baptism, confirmation, ordination, and healing. The sacraments cannot be enacted at a body-denying distance. They belong in a physical, celebrating assembly, with a presider and other ministers who serve that assembly.

- An electronic gathering too easily excludes. There are small congregations that cannot afford either the money or the time needed to procure and use electronic equipment. And there are people in our congregations who do not have internet access or internet skills. There actually is a "digital divide." "Discerning the body," as Paul puts the matter of attention to those who have been marginalized in 1 Corinthians, means paying attention to this potential exclusion. Furthermore, in our access to electronic media, we do not have to deal with people who are not like us or people we do not like. But Louis-Marie Chauvet is right: the primary form of church is the "diversified Sunday assembly" not just we as individuals or we and our family before a screen.
- There is a long and excellent tradition of the assembly finding ways to reach out to include people who are unable to be physically present. Sending the holy communion, however, always involves sending the ecclesial body—at least one communion minister representing the whole assembly—as well as the eucharistic body. The sacrament is not given to oneself in front of a computer screen, nor is it left in a bag at the door.
- A recorded liturgy too easily places the accent only on the presider and perhaps a few other ministers. Liturgy then becomes a thing to watch.
- A livestreamed liturgy or recorded liturgy with a congregation present runs the risk of sending out images of people's bodies without their permission. Liturgy needs to be done with profound respect for everyone present.

- People can quickly become weary of screen time. Doing church ought to give people a break, a rest from that work.
- We certainly are able to make electronic appeals for action toward social justice and for financial contributions for the hungry. But when a physical assembly includes a regular collection for the poor and when the whole event ends with the communal sending, our common identity as Christians together bearing witness in the world is made clear.
- Without being side by side with other bodies not our own, indeed without breathing together the same air and singing the same song, without the ancient kiss of peace that has marked the assembly, it is hard to see that we are one Body, enlivened by one Spirit.

Rather than continuing the emergency electronic means some of us have used when we needed to do so, we need now to recover and restore the biblical and liturgical reality of assembly. As we recover it, we need to teach its meaning and importance again.

In an article devoted to the recovery of common work in a physical office after the dangers of the pandemic have passed, Gianpiero Petriglieri, a professor of business ethics in France, wrote a few lines that are important for us as we think about assembly: "A self is what happens when culture meets flesh, and they always meet somewhere. Families, schools, churches, military academies, and, yes, offices, can be powerful identity workspaces. Those spaces don't just define us. They shape us. . . . They free us up, confine, mold, and repel us in various measures. It's easy to lose ourselves when we don't have a place, hate a place, or both." Petriglieri helps us see how important a place is to our identity, and the assembly is such a place. But churches too—assemblies—like some offices, can malform us. That is why, as we recover assembly and again find that identity, we need to keep working on reform. We need to help see that the culture that meets our flesh in that place—and meets the diverse flesh of others—is the culture proposed by Paul, articulated in the New Testament, and celebrated in the ecumenical liturgical movement. Assembly is not just a meeting; it is a meeting centered on the gospel of Jesus Christ and continually reformed to be the assembly of God. It is a place of shared communal ritual and symbol, of compassion and trust, and of the steady experience of material reality.

What might be characteristics of that ongoing reform? We will teach and teach what the New Testament and the liturgical movement have said about assembly. We will lay aside our electronic practices if they tempt us away from what we are teaching. We will rejoice in a personal communal gathering, a centered yet open gathering. We will read and preach the Scriptures with a full use of the ecumenical lectionary. We will celebrate the sacraments, "opening up" all the central symbols, to use Robert Hovda's phrase. There will be a Bath of water, a significant Book, a loaf of Bread, a full Cup of wine, and arms out in welcome and up in prayer. We will sing again. We will have a presider who knows how to serve the community and the dignity of each person. We will have many other ministers who also know this serving. We will seek to "discern the body," welcoming the very diversity that shows forth the primary form of church. We will seek to send and receive the instruments of communion: mutual aid and prayer for the other churches and for the poor; a recognized ministry; an ecumenically shared liturgy. We will be sent together to bear witness to the gospel for our neighbors and our place. We will repeatedly fail, but we will also know that while we together seek to act in assembly, prior to our action, underneath our action, God acts. In faith, we will trust that God has called us together around Christ and poured out the Spirit on our meeting.

When another pandemic inevitably comes, we will have sought to prepare all of us to pray and sing at home, as we once again, out of love for our neighbor, close our churches. We will have worked on learning again to sing. We will have made our church's worship resource a book for the home. We will have taught the lectionary and intercessory prayer. We will treasure the domestic church as a valuable memory of assembly. We will use the post, the telephone, or digital media to communicate, but perhaps we will not be quite so vulnerable to an electronic replacement for our being together.

Learning the assembly by heart—learning the spirituality of the assembly—will then include learning again the shared rituals and symbols we enact in assembly and the resonance of these things in daily life, learning the importance of recovered community, and regularly encountering the material reality of persons and place. That is a starting point in thinking about why assembly is so important.

Then we should think more about the sacraments in assembly, those quite specific symbolic rituals that have such a central role for us.

* * *

When I was a boy, even before I was a communicant according to the practice of my church in the late 1940s and early 1950s, my pastor made me an acolyte. I lit the candles before the service, of course, and I extinguished them afterward. But I also had a role in the sacraments. The small mission church to which we belonged—the Lutheran Church of the Redeemer, it was called—had no baptismal font. So I held the bowl that was used at baptisms, with a towel over my arm that the pastor could use to dry the head of a child newly baptized by sprinkling from that bowl. We also had no communion chalice. The communion wine was distributed, rather, by using small glasses, one given to each communicant. I stood inside the communion rail, and it was my task to pick up those glasses and put them on a silver tray.

These practices were by no means ideal. I would join those who today would long for a great font in which a child could be immersed, if possible, or a pool even, which could enable a full bathing also for adults. And I would hope that by now we have come to see not only that a common cup—a chalice—is the better symbol but also that it is the healthiest option. Still, I am grateful that I could be that close to baptisms and that I could see the communicants.

Seeing the communicants was stunning to me, maybe even life forming. I knew personally only a few, but there they all were, hands out together, like beggars. I could see their faces. Some were clearly glad. Some were actually weeping, and I remember especially my own stepfather, whom I thus came to see in a vastly different and more sympathetic light than was usually available to me. Some were keeping their reactions under more close control. But they were all there, together, hands out. At the center of this half-circle of mostly kneeling people stood the altar table, and on the table stood not just the linens and vessels of the Meal but also a crucifix. It was as if the sorrows and the hopes of that group of people were all being gathered up in the cross. In the common need of the communicants—in *our common need*, for I was included too—and in the common gift of God, we had together an important shared ritual symbolism and the deep basis for a community of trust. And I experienced, again and again, a level of human presence and human need seldom seen in daily life.

But it was not only me. My being close simply focused my youthful attention. Still, I came to realize that everyone who was there, if they looked, could see that reality: individual reactions yet communal action, a differentiated gathering of all sorts of people, profound human need and God's extended mercy, the meaning of the gift of Jesus Christ.

We need the assembly in order to see these things. When the pandemic began to close our churches in early 2020, a fine pastor I know was able to say in livestreamed sermons to her congregation that while they could not gather for the holy communion, they could remember it. The memory itself was and is a gift. She was right. Our gathering together with an assembly now builds on and continues to develop such memories. There are people who have no such memories, however, and now is the time to begin to form them. We will need those memories in moments of our own loneliness or, God forbid, when an even worse worldwide pandemic returns.

But when we have the unutterable gift of being free to assemble, we need to build securely the ground of those memories: profound shared rituals, a community for the incubation of trust, a steady taste of material reality, the assembly.

3

Why Are the Sacraments Assembly Events?

The meeting may then continue like this: Having concluded the Word part of the liturgy with mutual greetings of peace, the assembly begins to gather a collection and set the table for the Meal. Some members of the assembly begin to pass baskets around the room, gathering financial gifts intended to help people in need and to support the local and more-than-local ministries of the church. Other members take up a flagon of wine and a basket of fresh bread wrapped in a white cloth, along with the other gifts of food that have been brought. An assisting minister spreads a large square white cloth on the prominent table and places an empty cup on that cloth. Another assisting minister opens the great book of prayers and lays it too on the table. Meanwhile, the presiding minister and all the assisting ministers who will distribute the bread and cup to the assembly are thoroughly washing and drying their hands, in full view of the assembly. When all of this is prepared, the assembly stands as the cantor and the choir begin to lead everyone in singing a hymn or a part of a psalm appropriate to this moment. During the singing, the gifts of money, food, and specifically bread and wine are carried to the table. The basket full of the food to be given away is placed on the floor, in front of or beneath the table. The gifts of money are set on a small table to the side. The basket of bread and the flagon of wine are placed on the table itself. When the singing concludes, with the assembly still standing as they are able, one of the assisting ministers leads a prayer praising God, the source of all gifts, and begging God that these gifts may be used in the service of the gospel and the care of those in need. That same assisting minister then uncovers the bread in the basket on the table and pours wine into the cup. Then, as a central act in this liturgy, the presider comes to the table, exchanges sung greetings with the assembly, and adopting the orans *posture, begins to give thanks, singing an initial proclamation of praise. The assembly joins the song, using a text drawn from the account of Isaiah's inaugural vision and from Psalm 118, and the presider continues in a great prayer of thanksgiving, proclaiming the mercy of God, remembering Jesus's gift of himself in the supper as in his cross, resurrection, and presence in the assembly, and praying for the Spirit to make use of this Meal. The assembly repeatedly joins this thanksgiving with spoken or sung responses. Finally, the whole act of thanksgiving and prayer is summed up by the assembly together singing the Lord's Prayer. Especially during this last part—if not throughout the whole thanksgiving—many in the assembly themselves extend their arms in the old posture of prayer. The bread is then broken into baskets and the wine poured into as many additional cups as may be needed while the assembly sings to Christ as to the Lamb of God. The ministers then initiate the second central event in this part of the liturgy: standing at stations throughout the room, they distribute the holy Meal to people who come, hands extended, to receive the body and blood of Christ. Some ministers seek out at their chairs those who are not able to walk to a station. During all this time, the assembly sings hymns, texts that interpret what is happening. Only at the end do the ministers themselves receive communion, the presiding minister last of all. All are seated, the table is cleared, some of the bread and wine is set aside for those who are absent, and a silence follows. At last, the assembly rises again and sings the Song of Simeon, and an assisting minister prays a final prayer.*

Such is the third part of the ecumenical *ordo* for Sunday, the Meal. This third part may, of course, be done differently, but it ought always include a collection for those in need, a setting of the table, a great thanksgiving, and communal eating and drinking, with each person in the assembly being served by at least one other. That thanksgiving—*eucharistia* in Greek—gives its name to the whole event. This *eucharist* includes all the service—Gathering, Word, Meal, and Sending—as a single whole. But here the service centers especially on the communal enacting of that prayer of thanksgiving and the mutual sharing of the food of this thanksgiving.

Why Are the Sacraments Assembly Events?   57

In this present reflection on assembly spirituality, the Meal part of the service may remind us that the assembly is the home of the Christian sacraments. All of them. The sacraments, as these events are called in most of Western Christianity—or the *mysteria*, as they are called in the East—are assembly events. Why is that so? And what does it signify for practice and meaning?

One danger in Christian history has been that sacraments have sometimes been regarded as religious commodities, as spiritual goods for an individual to "get." The early centuries of Christianity saw some church leaders trying to prevent people from taking the food of holy communion home, not just so that they could commune themselves later in the week, which might have been permissible, but also so that they might, for example, plant the holy food along with their seeds so as to bless and increase their harvests or might carry that food on their persons for protection or good luck. Later centuries have seen people seeking to have their child "done"—baptized—even if such a ceremony had finally nothing to do with the religious teaching the child might receive or the life the child would live.

Some of this commodification of the sacraments had its source in one religious idea we have already seen: the understanding that Christianity was primarily about the salvation of individuals. In the midst of the group culture of the Middle Ages, such an accent on the individual may well have been salutary, providing a sense of both individual responsibility and individual freedom. In more recent times, however, focus on the salvation of the individual has often meant a neglect of social need. One result of a more careful and reforming reading of the Bible has been the liturgical accent on the assembly as the primary symbol of the people of God bearing witness now in the world. That accent does not mean that the individual is forgotten. Rather, the paradoxical truth of a faithful assembly is found in its being profoundly personal even as it is profoundly communal. Still, the old idea that sacraments are religious commodities for individuals to "get" has by no means disappeared.

The best resistance to such religious consumerism lies in the deep realization that the sacraments take place in assembly. Baptism is the washing that joins a person to the assembly of

Christians and to its mission in the world. The eucharist is the most regular observance of such an assembly, the sustaining Meal that the assembly shares, and its continual reorientation to life now in Christ. Both of these sacraments are assembly events. While they are graciously personal, they are not isolated things to be obtained by individuals. The same can be said for other matters that are sacramental in character or considered to be sacraments by some Christian communities. Confirmation is simply part of baptism, part of the constituting of the priestly people that gather as assembly. Absolution proclaims God's forgiveness and repeatedly reconciles the forgiven to the mission of the assembly, to the baptismal vocation. Ordination to ministry takes place not to increase the spiritual standing of individuals as individuals but in order to provide a company of serving leaders for assemblies. Anointing the sick is one way the assembly reaches out to those who cannot gather, a way that concretely signs the assembly's prayer. Even marriage, most often publicly blessed in a gathered assembly, is taken by some writers in the New Testament as an appropriate metaphor for the relationship between the assembly and Christ.

Learning the assembly by heart, we begin again to learn the sacraments by heart as assembly events. Taught by the paradoxical communal spirituality of the assembly, we come again and again to see the sacraments as personal while communal, centered while open, active while receptive realities. Our spirituality of the assembly will be deepened when we explore the sacraments as assembly events.

Baptism Constitutes Assembly

One of the great achievements of the twentieth-century liturgical renewal was the return of baptism to the assembled church. That return involved a significant recovery. Through the late Middle Ages and well into the modern era, baptism had become an increasingly private occasion. The baptism of adults had largely fallen away. Usually a family—or even only the parent or parents—gathered with their child and a single pastor or priest for the rite. Sometimes a sponsor or sponsors of the child were also there, though

Why Are the Sacraments Assembly Events?   59

these "godparents" were usually relatives, an extension of the family. Sometimes this gathering took place at the font in the parish church, though not at the time of the parish liturgy. But increasingly, as the centuries went on, it also took place in family homes. It was easy to regard such an event as an individual religious undertaking, the ritual solution to an individual problem. When baptism was taught to be simply the removal of the guilt of original sin from the soul, that teaching could be heard to underscore such an individual construal.

But that idea is not to be found in the New Testament. Rather, in the earliest Christian texts, to be baptized, as Paul would say it, is to be brought into Christ, to die with him, and to be made alive with him. All of us together who have been baptized, adults and children, are to walk in newness of life: *we*—a whole group—have been baptized into Christ (Rom 6:2–4). Being so baptized is to be "clothed . . . with Christ" (Gal 3:27). Separating distinctions between people are behind us; rather, "all of [us] are one in Christ Jesus" (3:28). Or, as the Synoptic Gospels image it, to be baptized is to be together with Christ in the water, under the same adopting voice from heaven and marked by the same Spirit, the sign of the arriving new age. Such a people is then sent together on mission, witnesses that God's new age is breaking into our world already now (Matt 3:16–17; 28:18–20). This community of witnesses, where the risen Christ abides, is "the church," the assembly (18:15–20; 28:20). Or, as the First Letter of Peter says, having been baptized, we are to "love one another deeply from the heart" (1 Pet 1:22), being then built together "into a spiritual house" (2:5), becoming "a royal priesthood, a holy nation, God's own people" (2:9), bearing witness to God's mighty acts for our neighbors in the whole world. We can rightly borrow the expression of Dietrich Bonhoeffer to understand all these New Testament texts: baptism brings the baptized into Christ-existing-as-assembly.

"Removal of the guilt of original sin," as medieval Christians in the West defined the primary benefit of baptism, is simply way too narrow and way too individual an understanding of the function of this washing as the New Testament presents it. Rather, it is better to say, as in the Lutheran document *The Use of the Means of Grace*, "In Holy Baptism the Triune God delivers us from the forces of evil, puts our sinful self to death, gives us new birth, adopts us as children, and makes us members of the body of Christ, the Church" (principle 14). Or, as one text for the rite of baptism in *Evangelical Lutheran Worship* has it, "God, who is rich in mercy and love, gives us a new birth into a living hope through the sacrament of baptism. By water and the Word God delivers us from sin and death and raises us to new life in Jesus Christ. We are united with all the baptized in the one body of Christ, anointed with the gift of the Holy Spirit, and joined in God's mission for the life of the world" (227).

That these definitions both involve the baptized being joined to a community, being made one with all the baptized, has also been expressed with many biblical metaphors. To be baptized is to join the people who in Christ have survived the flood (surely one of the meanings of the dove descending in the Gospel account of Jesus's baptism). To be baptized is to come with the people who cross the Red Sea to freedom. To be baptized is to be washed, anointed, and clothed as the ancient priests of the tabernacle were so prepared for their service (Exod 29:4–9). To be baptized is to be part of the church that was born from Christ's side when water and blood flowed out from the crucified (John 19:34–35). Or to be baptized is to come together with burning lamps in our hands to the wedding of God with the world (Matt 25:1–13).

More, the readings of the great Vigil of Easter give us a set of images for both what the resurrection of Christ means and what it means to be baptized into him. In baptism, we are together brought by the risen Christ into creation restored, into life after the flood, into freedom from sacrifice, and into participation in the people of the exodus. We are together given the water of grace, the bread and wine of wisdom, and new hearts in the place of hearts of stone. We are dry bones made alive together by the Spirit, a great host of people. Like Jonah, we are saved and called. We survive the fire like the three young men.

All these images mean to express that baptism makes us participants in the life of the new age of God, forgiven and not condemned, alive with Christ and not dead. All these images indicate that the baptized are made witnesses to grace, forgiveness, freedom, and life for the sake of the life of the world. And all these images indicate that this happens to each of the baptized as individuals and as an assembly. Baptism is a personal communal sacrament.

Baptism so understood has meaning for every day of our lives now and gathers us with every other member of the body of Christ into a vocation of love and service in the world now. Since baptism thus constitutes entry into Christ-existing-as-assembly, it rightly takes place in assembly.

Of course, there are exceptions. Though baptism is for life, it also can take place in the face of death as a fierce proclamation of life, *nonetheless*. A dying person may well not be able to come to the assembly. But a baptismal rite at a deathbed still will include as many members of the assembly as may easily come to the place where it occurs, and such a baptism will still be announced in the assembly. A congregation also may have a baptistry that does not accommodate the whole assembly. Still, the newly baptized will rightly be led directly into the assembly after the Bath by those assembly members and ministers who conducted the rite. The anointing, the prayer for the Spirit, the welcoming greeting of peace, and the participation in the supper will then take place in the full assembly. Or we may be again in the midst of a pandemic. In our recent experience of the widespread danger of infection, some baptisms were simply postponed until the assembly could safely and responsibly gather again. On the other hand, some newly born children may have been baptized by their own parents or other people with whom they lived. In that case, the best practice involved bringing those baptized children to the assembly as soon as it was possible and, once again, welcoming them with the prayer for the Spirit, the anointing, the signing with the cross, and their first communion. They, too, belong to the assembly.

But the home of baptism, the place where it situates us, is the assembly.

The significance of baptism taking place in assembly comes to expression in yet other ways. The preparation of adults for baptism—and adults' preparation to bring their children to baptism—can begin with a welcome rite and a signing with the cross in the assembly. In some baptismal rituals, parents and sponsors of children being baptized promise, among other things, to live with these children "among God's faithful people" and to "bring them to the word of God and the holy supper," as well as to catechetical instruction—in other words, to be with them in the assembly and its life—"so that [they] may learn to trust God, proclaim Christ through word and deed, care for others and the world God made, and work for justice and peace" (*Evangelical Lutheran Worship*, 228).

Also, many assemblies have begun not only to recover the standard practice of baptism in the assembly but also to appoint congregational sponsors to stand with the families of children and with adults as they come to baptism and join the assembly's life. Such a sponsor will have a role in the catechetical preparation of the candidate or the candidate's family before baptism and in the integration of the newly baptized into the ongoing mission of the assembly after the rite.

Furthermore, while baptism can take place in any water, it is a good thing for an assembly to have a font. That font ought not be a piece of furniture; it ought to be a *place*, a centering location in the assembly's space, grounding the assembly's space. Every time we gather, we come past it, remembering that we are baptized into Christ and so into the shared vocation of witness and service. It is best that the font be large, designed to accommodate a full use of water and, indeed, immersion in water when possible. Time and again, but especially at the great Vigil of Easter, we gather there to enact an affirmation of baptism. Baptism happens to individuals only once—"once for all," as it is said—as an all-encompassing and reliable gift. But it can be communally recalled by all of us together, again and again, as the one baptism we all share. Ordinations and marriages and prayers for people being sent in service from the assembly may all, at least in part, take place at the font. Funerals may begin there. And whenever absolution is proclaimed, it rightly is proclaimed from the font as a renewal of the gift and promise of baptism. Then, at least in many congregations, the leaders in the meeting—lay and ordained—wear the white garment that belongs to us all as the baptized. In helping us gather, in serving the assembly and its purposes, these ministers are exercising one version of the vocation given to us all in baptism.

Baptism finds its home in the assembly. It constitutes the assembly. Indeed, to learn the deep meanings of baptism by heart means to learn the assembly. Rich images for baptismal meaning and beautiful baptismal practice depict the experience as inviting and refreshing—like a bowl of clean, cool water on a hot day—welcoming those who are not baptized to consider coming and welcoming all who are baptized to see again what the assembly is. And baptism leads the baptized to holy communion; it is the Bath before the Meal. One could even say that eucharist is the repeatable part of baptism and that baptism and eucharist, the one-time Washing and the repeatable Meal, constitute a single thing.

Eucharist Is the Central Assembly Event

At first, it may seem obvious that the home of eucharist is also the assembly. Sunday eucharist and assembly are practically synonymous. Although many Protestant churches went through a long period in the eighteenth through the twentieth centuries when the full service of word and table was not celebrated very frequently, the late twentieth and early twenty-first centuries have seen a strong recovery of the Lord's Supper on the Lord's Day as the increasingly standard practice in every congregation. In those places, when one comes to church on Sunday, one expects the holy supper to be celebrated. That expectation was already the standard practice in Orthodox and Roman Catholic churches, even when the Word part of the eucharist was not so strongly observed in those communities.

Even so, the communal character of the eucharist—the assembly being the place where the sacrament belongs, the assembly as both the actor and the recipient in the holy Meal—was long obscured. In Roman Catholic churches, one frequently encountered the language usage that called the celebration of the sacrament "Father's mass." Indeed, the priest was frequently called "the celebrant," as if the *assembly* were not celebrating and as if the whole event belonged primarily to the priest. In both Roman Catholic and Orthodox circles, it was common for only a few people to commune. Rules about preparation, rules about pre-communion fasting, and the disallowance of anyone divorced and remarried actively discouraged a wide participation. A certain kind of piety, moreover, might have encouraged a person not so much to more frequent communion but to making an act of "spiritual communion" in which the person did not actually eat and drink but expressed in silent prayer a longing to do so. Moreover, although any Lutheran who knew the Small Catechism should have learned that "a person who has faith in these words, 'given for you' and 'shed for the forgiveness of sin,' is really worthy and well prepared" (*Evangelical Lutheran Worship*, 1166), the same low participation was notable in many Protestant churches. In some Scandinavian national churches, a person might have only communed twice in their entire life: at confirmation and again near death. Even in more recent times, with a Protestant recovery of eucharist every Sunday and Protestant, Roman Catholic, and Orthodox recovery of more frequent communion, the sacrament can still feel like a spiritual commodity that one "gets." The pastor or priest is often regarded as the purveyor of these holy goods—the one who makes or "confects" or "consecrates" them and the one who "administers" them—and the communicant is involved only to the extent that they receive what was administered.

Unfortunately, this widespread sense was in place when the latest coronavirus pandemic brought our churches to close. Decisions about what to do about eucharist in this time were then frequently driven by distorted preconceptions, and the question became simply, How can isolated people "get" communion? After the fact, we need not harshly judge decisions that were made in that time. Suddenly faced with a recently unprecedented question, local congregations and pastors did the best they could. And one should give thanks for the ways the people of congregations were able to stay in touch with one another and the ways that faith could still be fed.

But now it would be wiser to start again and rebuild, thinking more profoundly about eucharist and assembly. Say it clearly: the "celebrant" at the eucharist is not priest or pastor alone but the whole assembly, acting together. We all celebrate. Yet on, in, and under this communal celebration, the even more principal actor is God. The assembly receives God's gift and is turned toward the world, toward the neighbor, to serve as the assembly itself has been served. The eucharist gives us the principal example of participatory reception or receptive participation. Assembly, then—the bodily presence of a community in a concrete place—is the place where eucharist occurs, where it takes place. As Paul says in the very first account of the supper given to the church, "As often as you eat this bread and drink the cup, you proclaim the Lord's death until he comes" (1 Cor 11:26). The Greek *you* in this assertion is plural. It is *you all*, all the people keeping the Meal. The Lord's Supper, from the outset, was the Meal of the assembly, constantly converted by the Word of God to bear witness, in the power of the Spirit, to the crucified and risen Christ giving himself away.

When the meaning of this Meal is expressed in biblical metaphors, the communal character of the Meal is also never far away. The eucharist is then, for Christians, the manna and the water from the rock with which God feeds the people who have come across the sea. It is the repeated Passover meal in which the people together remember and eat from the Lamb whose blood saved them and set them free. Indeed, especially the story of the exodus has given Christians a connected narrative full of images that can express the way Water, Word, and the repeated Meal together form the assembly as a people of priests to bear witness to God's mercy for the life of all the world. But there are more images as well: eucharist is all of us eating with Abraham and Sarah's three visitors; all of us receiving Melchizedek's food of blessing; all of us—like Israel at Sinai—being marked with the blood of the covenant, beholding God, and eating and drinking in God's presence; all of us being fed by Jesus in the wilderness; all of us eating the fish meal by the sea. Or, to shift to the end of the Bible, eucharist is already the marriage feast of the Lamb and the eating from the tree of life with which the city of God is gifted. The metaphors are all richly communal.

The Lutheran tradition expressed this communal meaning and practice in this way in the mid-sixteenth-century formulation of the *Formula of Concord*, a text still regarded as confessionally authoritative among Lutherans: "But . . . the recitation of the Words of Institution of Christ by itself does not make a valid sacrament if the entire action of the Supper, as Christ administered it, is not observed. . . . On the contrary, Christ's command, 'Do this,' must be observed without division or confusion. For it includes the entire action or administration of this sacrament, that in a Christian assembly bread and wine are taken, consecrated, distributed, received, eaten, and drunk, and that thereby the Lord's death is proclaimed" (Solid Declaration, VII: 83–84). Note "in a Christian assembly" and "the entire action." Holy Communion is not made reliable and "valid" by clerical words alone but by Christ's gift and by that assembly in that entire action of celebrating and receiving that gift: a people in thanksgiving to God together with their presider, remembering and proclaiming the promise of Christ and then turning to the needs of their neighbors. Eucharist is not a thing to get but an event that happens in assembly and is enacted by an assembly.

The principal leader of this eucharistic assembly is rightly called "the presider," indicating the service that she or he gives to the meeting. That service is very important: the meeting needs to be led, lest it fall into confusion and disarray. The meeting needs to be loved and served, lest its purpose be missed. The meeting needs to be anchored in Christ and in the gospel, articulated and expressed by the presider in both preaching and praying. The meeting also needs to be in communion with other assemblies of Christians, and the recognized ministry of the presider is one of the instruments of that communion. The awareness, thus, that the entire assembly celebrates—the entire assembly enacts—the event of the eucharist is not an indication of lesser importance attached to the presider. On the contrary, although the presider does not own the eucharist and does not make it, the presider does have the important office of enabling the assembly to do its sacramental work. The manner of presiding should express that office: the presider faces the assembly across the table; cares about the people who are there and thinks of those who cannot be; holds bread and cup for the people to see but does not hover over these gifts nor handle them as if they belonged to the presider alone; and proclaims the eucharistic prayer with care and beauty, drawing the assembly into sharing that prayer.

This presider may be the called pastor of a local congregation. Or it may be the bishop of the synod or diocese to which the congregation belongs, perhaps supported by a college of presbyters or pastors or by the single local pastor. Or it may be a visiting pastor or bishop who is invited by the local congregation and to whom the local pastor graciously yields place.

But there are many other ministries to be carried out in the eucharist as well, many other ways the assembly is assisted in doing its work. One of the important recoveries of the renewal movement of the late twentieth and early twenty-first centuries has been the rebirth of these many ministries. Readers of Scripture, leaders of prayer, ministers of the Cup, members of the choir, doorkeepers or ushers all come from the assembly and help the assembly. These offices rightly belong to all the baptized, though an assembly also rightly looks for people with skills to read and sing and assist and then further seeks to train those skills. In some assemblies, a principal assisting minister, charged especially to set the table and lead the intercessions, may be a layperson. In others, this person may be an ordained deacon. The same may be true of the assembly's cantor or "leader of assembly song." But in any case, these persons need to be formed to lovingly serve and help enable the assembly's event.

Yet another of the most significant recoveries of the twentieth-century ecumenical practice of the eucharist, a recovery that has been especially important in articulating the assembly event, is the great thanksgiving at the table. At its best, this eucharistic prayer is a dialogue between the presider and the assembly. This prayer repeatedly speaks in the first-person plural: "we give thanks," "we proclaim," "we remember," "and we ask you . . ." The plural "we" is, of course, the assembly, in communion with all the assemblies. The prayer does not make the eucharist or offer it. Rather, it offers thanksgiving—"the fruit of lips that confess [God's] name" (Heb 13:15)—and it begs God to send the Spirit so that this Meal may form us to turn toward the needy world, "to do good and to share what you have" (13:16). The food, thus—the Bread and the Cup—is food of thanksgiving and beseeching before God. To eat and drink this food is for the assembly to join and indeed to *be* that thanksgiving and beseeching. And yet, in the mercy of God and the gift of the Sprit, the Bread and Cup are also and preeminently Christ giving himself to us, in body and blood, mercifully gathering us again into his body and turning us in him to give to our neighbor. In such turning, we enact how we have been made part of his self-giving.

This event of thanksgiving, eating, drinking, and being sent constitutes an assembly action. Yet all of it is received as a gift by an assembly. The event of the eucharist shows us a participatory receptive assembly. Also, individuals eat and drink. They are each served with honor and respect. Yet they eat and drink in community. They are gathered again into the body of Christ; the event of the eucharist shows us a personal communal assembly.

More, the thanksgiving, along with eating and drinking together, powerfully centers the assembly on Jesus Christ. Yet this very Jesus Christ is the one who identifies with the outsiders and the forgotten—with the needy world—and this Meal also sends its participants toward that world. The event of the eucharist shows us a centered, open assembly. The eucharist especially helps us learn by heart the paradoxical spirituality of the assembly.

The open assembly comes to expression in yet other ways. All are welcome to this table of God's mercy in Christ. The ordinary way to come to the communal eating and drinking runs through the equally welcoming Bath, runs through learning Christ and being washed into his body. Our assemblies should make that way clear, inviting, and available. On the other hand, sometimes someone will come first to the table, learning there, in that gift, who Christ is. Such access should not be refused, but the members of the assembly and their pastor should then make baptism available as the fitting response to that discovery and as the way of joining the assembly that keeps this Meal. Still, this is a *centered* open assembly: to come to both the Bath and the Table is to come to Christ and to find oneself dying in him as well as living. "Are you able to drink the cup that I drink," Jesus asks of his followers, "or be baptized with the baptism that I am baptized with?" (Mark 10:38). Jesus's cup and Jesus's baptism are, at their deepest, his cross. Both questions point to what Paul calls dying in Christ as well as being made alive in him. Baptism and eucharist are indeed open, but they are not cheap. They cost our lives.

The assembly also celebrates its open character by reaching out to those of its members who are unable to come—the sick, the hospitalized, the imprisoned, and those whose necessary work takes place at the Sunday hour when the assembly ordinarily meets. But such sending to the absent always includes not only the sending of the Bread and Cup, the communal food with which thanks has been given at the assembly's table, but also the sending of members of the assembly itself. These members will have been trained as visitors with the gospel of Jesus Christ and servers of his body and blood to beloved members. The assembly thus widens the circle, extending to include the absent as if they were part of that very Sunday's gathering. It is best, of course, if this sending takes place immediately after the eucharist concludes in the church, but if necessary, the bread and cup can be reverently reserved to be accompanied to the absent at a later time, as long as the food is not objectified as a commodity but is still thought of as part of a communal event that is still underway.

This sending also includes sending help to people who are in need. John Calvin was right to counsel that a Christian meeting should always include almsgiving. The eucharist classically has included an "offertory," a communal collection of food and money and a setting of the table with some of the food, while the rest is to be given away. Unfortunately, the convenience of electronic giving to the mission of the church and to charities has obscured this moment in many of our congregations. We would do well to recover the regular gathering of food for the hungry, the regular setting of the table by assembly members, and at least a symbolic collection of money—everyone who is able can put at least some money in an offering plate, though their major giving is electronic. Such reflections can help make more clear for us why participation in a eucharist by watching someone preside in a livestreamed or recorded liturgy contributes to a significant decay in sacramental meaning.

Thus, the eucharist finds its home in the assembly as the central assembly event. Learning this eucharist by heart will be learning the assembly by heart.

Other Sacramental Events Express and Serve the Assembly

Something quite similar can be said about the home of other matters that have been regarded as sacraments or, at least, as sacrament-like or sacramental. There is no need for Christians to quarrel about how many sacraments there are. Baptism and eucharist—along with the reading and preaching of the Scriptures and prayer for the needs of the world—stand at the center of the life of the assembly. But other matters are important, circling around that center. Seeing all these actions as part of assembly life can be one way to learn the assembly by heart.

People are absolved—in communal or individual confession and forgiveness—in order to reconcile them to the assembly's purpose and restore them again and again to Christian life for the sake of the life of the world. Sometimes that absolution takes place in the assembly itself in a way that recalls and renews the promise of baptism—it is a kind of creeping back to the baptismal Bath for all of us. Sometimes it takes place individually, the penitent with a pastor, though then too it may occur at the font or in the usual meeting room of the local assembly. Sometimes it takes place in the mutual conversation and consolation of members of God's family with one another, people showing each other grace in the midst of ordinary life. But in every case, those who are forgiven can be understood as rejoining the assembly's mission to be priests for the sake of the life of the world, to be themselves signs of forgiveness.

Then people are ordained in order to serve the assembly in the ministry of presiding or in the ministry of diaconal service. The former involves especially preaching in the assembly and presiding at baptism and eucharist, the core events that constitute and express the assembly's purpose. When such a pastor is elected and appointed as a bishop, it may also involve presiding in that form of church that exists as a communion of assemblies, as a synod or diocese, and that presiding too will be focused on preaching, teaching, and eucharistic leadership, not simply on administration. The call to diaconal service may include a function in the meeting—as cantor or reader of the gospel or leader of intercessory prayer—but it may also and especially involve care for the sick and the poor in a needy world, a care that expresses outreach from the meeting and from its intercessions. The call to assembly service thus represents a transformation of a simple appointment of leaders to be something more profound: one way the assembly models that all Christians are being conformed to the life of Christ the Servant. Ordination is not a thing that an individual "gets" but an expression of the community's need. Ordination always involves assembly and should take place in assembly.

Why Are the Sacraments Assembly Events? 71

More, the sick are visited and prayed for as an extension of the assembly's prayer. That extension sometimes involves anointing for healing, sometimes simply praying, and sometimes bringing communion as an extension of the assembly's table. And even marriage seeks to found a small community that in its hospitality, service, and mutual forgiveness will echo something of the mission of the assembly itself.

In all of this, the root sacrament is the presence of Christ in the assembly. Or, to say the matter with Louis-Marie Chauvet, the assembly—when it is faithful to the gospel—constitutes the "fundamental sacrament of the risen Christ." That presence, on, in, and under all of these quite physical actions, is what a spirituality of the assembly most seeks to learn by heart.

* * *

When the Episcopal cathedral in Philadelphia was reconsecrated after a considerable remodeling, the Lutheran bishop in Philadelphia was invited to participate. One characteristic of the newly designed worship space was a large font, a kind of stone trough full of water, incorporating the old font in the corner as a water source and, because of the massive extent of the water the trough contained, fully enabling the immersion baptism of adults. There was to be a baptism in the course of this reconsecration, and since—as an ecumenical gesture—local Lutherans had contributed substantially to the cost of the construction of this font, the Lutheran bishop was to preside at this baptism. He asked me to assist him as a kind of chaplain. The catechesis and preparation of the candidate for baptism had taken place in her congregation, a largely Tagalog-speaking, Filipino Episcopal church that held their liturgies in the cathedral. We had not ourselves met the candidate until we met her at the font in the midst of the liturgy. At the time for the baptism, she came to the font, accompanied by many of the people of her congregation, her regular assembly. I was more than a little worried when I saw her. The bishop and I were expecting that she would be immersed in this pool—that is, that she would kneel in the water in the midst of the trough while the bishop poured water over her. But here she came, wearing an elegant black dress, a string of pearls, and high-heeled shoes. What were we to do?

Not to worry. She knew what she was doing. At the time of the baptism itself, she deftly kicked off her shoes and, aided by the members of her assembly who were with her, graciously stepped over the edge of the pool and knelt in the water, black dress and all. The baptism took place. Then her congregation helped her out, wrapping her in a great towel and taking her to the sacristy. There, while the large assembly in the cathedral was being sprinkled by both bishops with water from the font, she could dry off and change from her wet clothes into a white alb. She was then again accompanied by people from her congregation as she came out to meet the Episcopal bishop at the cathedra (the bishop's great chair) in the assembly space just as he was returning from scattering the water. The liturgy continued with her being anointed with chrism by the bishop and being presented to the whole assembly.

What I remember most from this striking event was not only this woman's remarkable poise and confidence but the company of her equally poised and confident congregation. Her assembly brought her to the water, welcomed her from the water, brought her to the bishop, and welcomed her into life in Christ in the church. That baptism was overwhelmingly an assembly event.

Around the edge of that Philadelphia font, these words from the Revelation to John are inscribed in the stone: "The angel showed me the river of the water of life . . . flowing from the throne of God and of the Lamb through the middle of the street of the city" (Rev 22:1–2). I saw the water of life flowing there, in that assembly, for that city.

Another story: When one of my sons was three and four years old, he used to play church. By that time, he was already a communicant, and holy communion was clearly the event in church—along with sung intercessions—that most clearly caught his imagination. So when he wanted to play church, he would usually get my attention and then sing a few bids, to which I was expected to reply with a sung "Lord have mercy." Then he would take a piece of bread, break it, and put the broken piece in my hand, solemnly saying, "Grace Lutheran Church," which had been the name of our congregation. Of course, I would have been glad if he knew the actual words used during communion, but he was only three and four! And the more I thought about it, the more I thought he was also quite right in his playacting what the assembly does. When Christ gives us himself, we are given all those who are in him. We are given the assembly.

4

How Does the Assembly Form Us for Daily Living?

Finally, the meeting may come to its conclusion in this way: Simeon's Song, in which everyone asks to be dismissed in peace, has been sung. An assisting minister has led everyone in a prayer after communion. The assembly then sees several of its members come to the table once more. There these people, commissioned to be ministers of communion to the sick and the absent, receive beautiful wooden boxes that contain some of the bread and wine that has been part of the Meal here today. The presider prays for these people who are being sent, the assembly assents with an amen, and they leave directly to go to those who, though necessarily absent, have asked to receive communion today. Then a few announcements are made about events in the following days that will engage the assembly or some of its members in care for the surrounding world. The presider speaks a blessing, and an appropriate final hymn is sung, during which the assisting ministers and the presider follow the cross to the font. There the principal assisting minister speaks words of dismissal, and the assembly replies with "thanks be to God." Everyone leaves. They go individually or in family groups, but they also go marked by what they have been and done together here. On the way, many pass the font, again touching the water and marking their foreheads with a cross.

This very brief enacting of the fourth section of the ordinary outline of Christian Sunday liturgy—or something very much like what is described here—makes up the Sending. As we have done with the other three parts of the liturgy in the preceding chapters, we may use the Sending for further reflection on the spirituality of assembly, this time thinking about the ways the assembly and its practice can form us for living outside of the meeting. Assembly around Jesus Christ and his gospel, assembly in the triune name, does have meaning for daily life.

We may see that meaning more clearly if we begin by considering again the liturgical structure that leads to the Sending. The pattern of the Sunday eucharist ordinarily involves four pillars or four juxtaposed movements: the Gathering, the Word, the Meal, and the Sending. Sometimes this shared *ordo* is interpreted by reference to the Emmaus story in Luke 24: we gather with the risen One, like those disciples on the way; we hear the scriptural word, "beginning with Moses and all the prophets" (Luke 24:27), interpreted as about Christ; in the "breaking of the bread," we encounter with burning hearts the one who is at the center of this opening of the Scriptures; and then we run back to the city—we go to our city, our neighborhood—to tell what we have seen. Gathering, Word, Meal, Sending.

Sometimes, instead, this structure is seen in Justin Martyr's second-century account of the Christian Sunday meeting as written in his *First Apology*, an account that has been important to the modern ecumenical liturgical renewal movement. Like Justin's community, we gather together in one place, remembering that we are baptized; a reader reads the Scriptures, and our presider in preaching invites us to understand ourselves and our world in the pattern of what has been read; we stand and pray for the needy world; then bread and a cup of wine are brought, and that same presider gives thanks as well as he or she can, proclaiming Christ's gift; we eat and drink that gift, sending the food also to community members who are sick, in prison, or detained; and we take a collection of food and money for the wretched poor who live all around us, sending that help though the hands of the presider and others who help. Eucharist is sent to the absent, help is sent to the poor, the assembly itself is sent. So this fourfold event—Gathering, Word, Meal, Sending—makes up the event of the eucharist, the central event of the Christian assembly. Learning that fourfold shape by heart will mean learning the assembly by heart.

What has been especially new to our time in this structural outline is the recovery of the Sending. Called by different names in our churches—Sending, the Sending Out, the Dismissal—it is no longer simply a conclusion, closing off the liturgy with a benediction as if the service were an entirely interior event, with nothing else supposed to happen. The Sending rather recovers the old directive *Ite, missa est* called out by a deacon in the classic Western Christian liturgy. That phrase meant literally "go, it is sent"—the idea being that the whole liturgical event has prepared a people to go and that the benediction that immediately preceded this dismissal was originally the bishop's blessing on those who were indeed going, to guard them on their way. *Ite, missa est* may have originally meant simply, on the example of court ceremony, "go, it is the dismissal." Or it may have meant "go, the bread is sent"—that is, some of the food of the eucharist is sent as a sign of communion with the other churches (in what was called the *fermentum*). Or, remembering Justin, it may have meant "the food or help for the poor is sent." Or, most basically and finally, it has come to mean "go, the church is sent." Indeed, in the later Middle Ages and then today in Roman Catholic and some Anglican and Lutheran circles, including all of Lutheran Scandinavia, that dismissal has lent its name to the whole eucharistic rite: *missa*, mass, *mässa* it is called, as if the eucharist is, as a whole, a Sending. And it is.

Many contemporary liturgical formulations give words to that Sending—a Dismissal or a Charge—final words in the mouth of an assisting minister or deacon, spoken to the assembly to mark the people's transition to a needy world. These words can be simply "go in peace," as in the Roman Mass, or "go in peace to love and serve the Lord," as in Church of England and American Episcopalian use. Or, in language borrowed from the French Huguenots, who were among the earliest to recover the liturgical Sending, doing so in a way that reflected Paul in Galatians 2:10, the words can be one of the options found in the current *Evangelical Lutheran Worship*: "Go in peace. Remember the poor." The same book has the quite simple promise, "Go in peace. Christ is with you." Or the sending words can be more extensive. One alternative Charge in the 2018 *Book of Common Worship* of the Presbyterian Church (USA) uses these other words from Paul: "Love one another; serve the Lord; live peaceably with all" (Rom 12:10–11, 18). The 2009 text of the Eucharist of the Anglican Church of Ceylon has the deacon say,

"Brothers and sisters, to the mercies of the glorious Trinity we commit you, go now in the food of your pilgrimage in peace and gladness. Serve the Lord and help to free others." The yet longer words of Sending from the Oslo City Mission of the Church of Norway both send and invite return:

> Go! Never stop going out from church, out from peace and stillness, out into noise and discomfort, out to tears and laughter. Carry with you the living bread that you were given here, as a treasure between your hands and in your heart, and share it again and again. It will suffice forever, as long as you continue to break it. Come! Never stop coming back to this place. Never come with empty hands. Bring with you the cry that is pressing behind your lips. Let it sound here. Bring with you the hunger that is never stilled, the fight that is not yet won. Bring with you one who has always been at your side, without you knowing it. Here is the meeting place, in the light of the face of God.

In a quite similar way, the 2004 Outline Order for Holy Eucharist of the Church in Wales, reworking material from the 1989 New Zealand Anglican Prayerbook, recalls the gifts of the whole liturgy itself as turning us toward the Sending. A dialogue between minister and assembly first blesses God for what has happened in this meeting—"Blessed be God who calls us together . . . forgives our sin . . . whose word is proclaimed . . . whose grace is abundant"—and then says, "Accept, O Lord, our thanks and praise." The assembly responds, "Our hands were empty until you filled them." The minister continues, "We will serve the Lord." And the final assembly response is "in the name of Christ. Amen." Such a Sending enacts the whole eucharist as mass, *missa*, *mässa*.

In other words, it is not simply the Sending that sends us or releases us for mission. It is the whole gift of God enacted in the assembly's liturgy, the Spirit of God poured out there and turning us outward. Word and sacrament in the assembly can be seen as God going out in love toward all the needy world and gathering us along in that very mission. Forgiveness in the assembly turns us as ministers of forgiveness to others. The word of God in the assembly gives us truth and good news to share and images to interpret our common world. The Meal in the assembly turns us toward the hungry others, to be ourselves as bread. We need to continue to think about how the events of the liturgy thus mark us and form us for daily living. Indeed, enacting these events publicly already belongs to the mission of God in the world, and a Sending is hard to imagine without these events forming its content.

Christianity is a communal phenomenon, and Christian life ought especially to be formed by this meeting. Once again, this assertion ought not bring us to idealize the community. On the contrary, the Christian assembly understands itself rightly as a gathering of beggars, of people in need of forgiveness and grace, and—when the event is faithful—forgiveness and grace are indeed given in the meeting. But the need with which we came must not be forgotten. It is not that the group itself is all that wonderful, and Christian spirituality ought not be the shared illusions of a self-important group. Rather, the central matters of the assembly—the central things that bear that forgiveness and grace to us—do shape us if we let them, as we frequently do not. Let that be said honestly and clearly: Christians frequently do not live out the vision they communally enact in their meeting, even and perhaps especially when that meeting is faithful. Still, the vision is there. Though we go from the meeting individually—personally—the communal identity can mark our days. That we have been honest about our need together and that we have together rejoiced in God's gifts can form how we each live in the world, often apart from one another but still engaged in a shared vocation that we saw together and found renewed in the assembly.

Living from the Word and Prayer

Martin Luther gave us one way to consider how hearing the word of God may form us for daily living. In his introduction to the *Church Postil*, the collection of sermons he published in 1522, Luther argued that when the Gospel book is read and preached, we should know that Christ is here, coming to us or we being brought to him, present in the reading and preaching, and doing to us now what the text says he did then: forgiving us, healing us, raising us from the dead. Luther then continued, "If you pause here and let him do you good, that is, if you believe that he benefits and helps you, then you really have it. Then Christ is yours, presented to you as a gift. After that it is necessary that you turn this into an example and deal with your neighbor in the very same way, be given also to him as a gift and an example." That "it is necessary" ought not be heard as a demand. Rather, faith that trusts the gift of Christ simply must become, as Paul says the matter in Galatians, "faith working through love" (Gal 5:6). Faith, when it is authentic, turns to the needs of the neighbors. If the God in whom a believer trusts is the Creator and Redeemer of all, then that trust will carry within itself the necessity of turning in care toward what has been created and redeemed. Of course, such giving to others as Christ has given to us by no means always happens. But our repeated return to the assembly and thus our repeated hearing of the gospel does form us and forms us all together. Being honestly the sinners forgiven, the sick healed, the dead raised—as we are all together in the assembly—inevitably calls for being with other people in the world in a way marked by humility and love. That way is a path and vocation given to all Christians whether or not we follow it. How exactly that vocation is lived out is not prescribed. We all have many different ways to go, remarkably different gifts, and a rich diversity of tasks and contexts for service. But the assembly shares in the central call given to us all together when we hear the gospel. Our true identity is to be the body of Christ, given away—"gift and example," as Luther says—whether or not we live from our true identity.

Or we might articulate how the Word forms us by listening again to Justin. When the reader of the Scriptures finishes, Justin writes, "the presider in a discourse admonishes and invites us into the pattern of these good things." Whatever else the pattern of the good things of the Scriptures is, it is at least this: the very shape of God's acting to save; the repeated story of failure and hope, sin and forgiveness, death and life, dry bones enlivened by the Spirit—the story with which the Bible is full; and especially this death and life summed up in the presence of the crucified and risen Jesus Christ. When preaching is faithful, the preacher is inviting the assembly into this pattern in order to understand the world and ourselves. Using biblical images for our failure and need admonishes us. Proclaiming the mercy of God in Christ invites us. Trusting this Word, being brought by God's Spirit "into" its pattern, is called "faith," and in faith, the very death-and-life pattern of the Scriptures is replicated. By the power of the Spirit, we who are dead are made alive together with Christ. Our assembly, like Justin's, needs this encounter with the heart of the Scriptures again and again. Then it will be no surprise that our assembly, formed in this Word like Justin's assembly, will also send eucharist to the absent and help to the poor. The biblical "life" that follows the biblical "death" in the pattern of the Scriptures must necessarily involve life for the world.

In the Sunday eucharist, yet another way we can see how hearing the Word turns us toward our neighbor and our needy world is found in the intercessions. When the Scripture reading and preaching have concluded, the assembly responds by turning to prayer. One outline for these prayers says that they should "reflect the wideness of God's mercy for the whole world," including prayers

> for the church universal, its ministry, and the mission of the gospel;
> for the well-being of creation;
> for peace and justice in the world, the nations and those in authority, the community;
> for the poor, oppressed, sick, bereaved, lonely;
> for all who suffer in body, mind, or spirit;
> for the congregation, and for special concerns.

These prayers should conclude with thanksgiving for those who have died, including those commemorated on the church's calendar. This is a full list and one that should regularly be filled out locally and currently with attention to what is happening in the world and in the local neighborhood that calls for our prayer. Too often, these intercessions—this "prayer of the faithful," these beseechings of the assembly—have been neglected in our liturgies; they have been shallow, focused only on ourselves, or even omitted. The list can call us to a deeper practice. Still, it should also be remembered that this list is a list for genuine prayer—for standing before God as delegates or priests for the sake of others—not an agenda for our communal action. Such prayer arises out of faith in the biblical God, faith that God cares and acts.

Nonetheless, if we pray in such a way, our imagination about the needs of the world—our sense of how to understand the world—will be deepened with compassion. And we will walk in the world with that imagination and compassion refreshed. Again, the specifics of our action are not spelled out. But the character of our assembly vocation becomes clearer simply by our praying together. Intercession may then form a way to walk in the world, perhaps by our quietly praying for everyone we meet, perhaps by our bringing with us to the assembly's prayers when we gather again a memory of whatever agonies we have seen, but mostly by our being communally formed to see the world under God's mercy and to turn from hearing the gospel to giving such care for our neighbor as we can give, just as the liturgy itself turns from proclamation of the Scripture to intercessions.

But there is not only intercession—or beseeching—in the assembly's meeting. There is also thanksgiving. In fact, the regular pattern of Christian prayer involves a kind of double helix of thanksgiving and beseeching wrapped around each other, answering each other, often correcting each other. The world is not only filled with aching need; it is also filled with stunning gift. Christian liturgy specifically sees that gift while also specifically seeing the overwhelming need. Thanksgiving is present in liturgy at the start of every brief prayer, at the end of the intercessions, as the major content of prayer over the font and prayer at the table, and as the name—the *eucharist*—we often use for the whole Sunday event. And such thanksgiving also forms us, widens our imagination, deepens our genuine hope. Such thanksgiving may also be a way to walk in the world, perhaps by our quietly giving thanks for everyone and everything we meet, perhaps by our bringing a memory of such brilliant gifts with us when next we give thanks with the assembly at the table, but mostly by our being formed with the assembly to live thankfully in our daily lives.

Assembly practice of Word and Prayer, a practice to learn by heart, thus can form us and send us.

Living from Baptism and Eucharist

Martin Luther also gave us a way to imagine how coming to communion might form us for daily living. In his 1519 essay or sermon on "The Blessed Sacrament of the Holy and True Body of Christ," Luther used the idea of the *admirabile commercium*, the remarkable or, as he called it, *joyful* exchange, which is the very commerce of the city of God. Christ in the supper takes our need and loss and sin upon himself and gives us his own blessedness. The supper is God in Christ in the power of the Spirit coming toward us and giving himself away to us. So we, baked into one loaf with Christ and all the saints and, indeed, all the wretched of the world, are to turn to our neighbor:

> When you have partaken of this sacrament, therefore, or desire to partake of it, you must in turn share the misfortunes of the fellowship. . . . Here your heart must go out in love and learn that this is a sacrament of love. As you experience love and support, so in turn you give it to Christ in his needy ones. You must feel . . . all the unjust suffering of the innocent, with which the world is everywhere filled to overflowing. You must fight, work, pray, and—if you cannot do more—have heartfelt sympathy. . . . Thus, in the sacrament . . . Christ takes us upon himself and acts in our behalf as if he were what we are, taking up what concerns us as if it were his concern, taking it up even more than we do. In turn, we also wish to take Christ upon ourselves, as if we were what he is, which indeed will finally happen—we shall be conformed to his likeness. . . . Thus our sins assail him, while his righteousness protects us. For the union makes all things common until at last Christ completely destroys sin in us and makes us like himself, at the Last Day. Likewise by the same love we are to be united with our neighbors, we in them and they in us.

Thus Luther's interpretation of the celebration of the holy supper is much like his understanding of the reading and preaching of the Gospel book. In both, we encounter the amazing exchange, and that exchange forms us for daily living. God in Christ giving to us does not so much lead to our giving back to God but to our giving to our neighbor or giving to God by giving to our neighbor. The direction of this "commerce," this exchange, is all outward with the mission of God. Participation in the sacrament should be followed by at least that "heartfelt sympathy." Walking in the world, formed by the assembly's sacrament of love, formed in sympathy, may well then lead to "you must fight, work, pray" when the world is so filled with sorrow. Again, this is not a demand; it is simply a description of what faith in conformity to Christ and the Spirit, faith active in love, is like. Nor is it a specific description of what Christians will do. Rather, it is a way the members of the assembly are marked by one of their central practices.

Something similar can be said about baptism. The baptismal Bath and its regular remembrance—events that take place in the meeting—identify the assembly with Jesus Christ, with his death and his resurrection, and with the Spirit poured out from him. Baptism leads to life in Christ. But Jesus Christ is the one who identifies with the littlest ones, with outsiders and sinners, with the least and the poorest. Thus far from baptism distinguishing a chosen people set over against all the others—a pure people, untouched by the impure—baptism rather constitutes an assembly that is identified in Christ with all the others. Baptism is the Bath that makes us dirtier, immersed in the needy world. "Once you were not a people," says the First Letter of Peter, "but now you are God's people" (1 Pet 2:10). And that new identity is not intended to take this people away from the needy world. On the contrary, "Once you had not received mercy, but now you have received mercy." Such mercy is to be given away.

Again, there are no clear specifics in this assembly vocation. "Love one another; serve the Lord; live peaceably with all," as one charge in the *Book of Common Worship* says. Or "remember the poor," as the Huguenots and the American Lutherans say, where "remember" does not simply mean "think about" but "take seriously," "shape your life toward," "take a collection to help," and "take action to resist the structures that lead to such poverty." Or, with Luther, "fight, work, pray." Or, with Paul, "contribute to the needs of the saints; extend hospitality to strangers," and "owe no one anything, except to love one another" (Rom 12:13; 13:8). The second major part of Paul's letters—the *parainesis* or ethics-recommending part, the part that follows the gospel that fills the first part of the letter—frequently contains such counsel as found in these phrases from Romans. Similarly, the Spirit of life and mercy poured out on the assembly in its meeting has fruits to be born in daily life: "love, joy, peace, patience, kindness, generosity, faithfulness, gentleness, and self-control" (Gal 5:22–23). And as we shall see when we consider the catechism in chapters 5 through 8, baptism brings with it a baptismal ethics.

Thus assembly practice of baptism and eucharist, practices to learn by heart, can also form us and send us.

There is, of course, more to be said. We have already considered how the assembly's language use may open us to metaphoric rather than literal speech, how its attention to place and time and bodies can keep us focused on material existence, how its diverse community may help us imagine a more diverse world, and how its reading of different scriptural voices side by side can help us resist ideology. If the assembly we know is indeed marked by the paradoxes of personal/communal, centered/open, and participatory/receptive, these very tensions can influence how we live: communally engaged yet respectful of individual persons, committed yet open minded, active yet humble about what we can accomplish. The focal practices of the assembly, as we have seen in chapter 3, have implications for daily life, especially if the symbols are made larger and more engaging. The assembly's care about words can form a person for lifelong care about words. That the central practice of the assembly includes a Meal can form participants to regularly give thanks at table, care about the food, and share their food in hospitality to others. Of course, the primary "formation" that takes place in a faithful assembly is the formation in faith, the return—again and again—to trusting the biblical and triune God. And such trust turns us in daily life toward the needs of our neighbor and the needs of the life of the world.

Living toward the Next Catastrophe

But there is one more formation we need to consider. In recent history, our churches have had to shut down the face-to-face, in-person, bodily assembly. We have had to enter such a fast from essential Christian practice because of an even more essential devotion, a devotion to the well-being of the community and the health of the neighbor. In a pandemic, bodily gathering—breathing and speaking and singing with a group of people in the same space—was simply too dangerous, too easily and insidiously a spreading place for a virus that could, as we sorrowfully learned, kill the vulnerable. As we have come back to participation in assembly, we need to be prepared to stop again. There will be more viruses. Such an awareness is not about giving in to depression; it is simply open-eyed wisdom.

There will also be other catastrophes. Climate change threatens to bring with it yet more mass migrations of people from the Global South toward the North and from seacoasts toward interior land, all in the search for food and life. Even without these migrations, continued poverty will continue to bring large-scale food insecurity. We are not, alas, done with wars—nor with natural disasters: earthquakes, volcanic eruptions, tsunamis, hurricanes, tornadoes, fires, floods. As we pray in the assembly for the needs of the world, we should be formed to be aware of all of these and, in response, to do what we can to help, including working to influence responsible governmental and national engagement with these emergent needs.

Usually, however—unless the catastrophe is local and very serious—these events will not close down our assembly gatherings. But another worldwide pandemic will bring us to close again, and we need to be prepared.

One of the things the assembly can do now is practice better hygiene in the current time. Viruses and other pathogens are always present. There is a certain risk in simply gathering as a group at all—though there is also a decided risk in not gathering, in being isolated from others and from the essential central assembly practices we have been considering here. So wisdom and care are called for. Presiders and the ministers of communion can wash their hands well. So can everybody who comes to church. Members

How Does the Assembly Form Us for Daily Living?   85

of the assembly may consider exchanging the sign of peace by means of a bow or the grasping of forearms or the use of the Indian *namaste* or the Thai *wai* rather than by a handshake. Communion by means of intinction—with communicants dipping the communion bread into the cup before eating—should be abandoned altogether, all those hands being put into the cup being the least clean method available to us. The many hands that touch the edge of the small glasses some congregations use may also lead an assembly to abandon that method as well. Instead, a common cup, held by only one person and carefully cleaned after each communicant drinks or fitted with a pouring lip and used to pour into single-use or personally brought small glasses, may continue to be our wisest practice.

But there may be a time again when the assembly must not gather at all. By a strong and faithful assembly practice now, we may be able to form enough experience of the assembly that—at least for those people who are able to do so—a reversion to electronic means of being in touch with one another will be able to build on that memory.

There is, however, more to be said. We need to let our assembly practice so form us that we can echo that practice in our own homes in a kind of domestic church. We need so to learn the assembly by heart that we will be able to continue parts of the assembly away from one another while still remembering and praying for one another. It would, for example, be a good thing if the worship book our assembly regularly uses were a book we all had at home, if people knew how to use the calendar and find the lectionary readings for any Sunday, and if people had been helped to sing hymns at home. A congregation could build a sense of unity and connection—even without any electronic connection—by sending to every member an outline of Sunday prayers: the prayer of the day, the lectionary readings, perhaps a written sermon, perhaps locally crafted intercessions, and suggested hymns. This outline could include a suggested time on Sunday when the members of the congregation would undertake to use these prayers with a sense of doing this together while nonetheless separated. Even without that congregational planning, however, a person living alone or people living together could be helped to know their way through the worship book and thereby have a sense of wider connection: using the church's lectionary; singing the church's hymns; keeping the church's feast and commemoration days; and possibly learning again to pray the church's daily offices of Morning Prayer, Evening Prayer, or Compline. All these things can be done at home, led by one of us or several of us, without needing an ordained minister. We can also find ways safely to make contributions from home of food and money for people in need and financial support for the church, another of the assembly's central practices that we will need to continue.

The sacraments, which as we have argued have their home in the gathered assembly, are of course another matter. They will not take place in the domestic church. Still, their echo will be there. Baptism can be remembered. And, in need, anyone can baptize, and then—when the assembly can gather again—the person baptized can be received, publicly prayed for or anointed, and welcomed to the table. More, if the assembly's practice has been learned by heart, our own tables of daily food will echo something of the Lord's Supper, especially when our tables are marked by thanksgiving and by sharing. One table prayer has it this way:

> Come Lord Jesus, be our guest,
> and let these gifts to us be blessed.
> Blessed be God who is our Bread.
> May all the world be clothed and fed.

The domestic church is not the place for the full eucharist. But it is indeed the place for the presence of Jesus Christ, crucified and risen and alive to us in the reading of the Scriptures and in prayer in his name. Jerome is reputed to have once said, "We eat the flesh and drink the blood of the divine Savior in the holy eucharist; but so do we in the reading of the Scripture." And Luther—who in his "Babylonian Captivity of the Church" quoted Augustine as saying, "Believe, and you have eaten"—then himself added, "Therefore, I can hold mass every day." When, out of love for our neighbor, we need to close the assembly and its weekly eucharist again, we will need to remember these witnesses.

An assembly, in encouraging its meaning and practice to be learned by heart, will wisely and peacefully also be preparing for the next catastrophe.

*   *   *

Often, when trying to teach a seminary class about the central matters of Christian worship, I would use an old Danish bell inscription to do so. "To the Bath and the Table, to the Prayer and the Word, I call every seeking soul," the inscription read, as if thereby telling us what the sound of the bell was saying in the village where it rang. I love that inscription. It names most of the matters we have been considering here: baptism and eucharist, word and prayer. And everybody in need—"every seeking soul"—is invited. One time, however, I mistakenly pointed out what was not there in that list. In the hearing of Mark, the excellent seminary musician with whom I worked, I said, "No music, Mark!" Without skipping a beat, he replied, "Gordon, it's a bell!" He was right, of course, and I was wrong. A bell makes that invitation, and it thereby signals that the event to which it invites us is itself all music. The Bath, the Table, the Prayer, and the Word all occur with the assembly singing. The whole event—Gathering, Word, Meal, Sending—is musical. And Song is one of those focal practices that form us for walking in the world. Indeed, as we seriously prepare for another time when we might have to let in-person meeting go, we need to work on all of us once again singing. That recovery will be against the current cultural practice, against the way that the ready availability of recorded or digital song has silenced our own voices, against the shaming that so many adults remember about how their own voices and their own abilities "to carry a tune" have been received by others, sometimes especially their teachers. But that central characteristic of the assembly—that glad use of singing—also needs to be learned by heart. And a good cantor can help almost anyone sing.

The people who answer the bell's invitation are all needy, "every seeking soul." Consider another image: all over the interior walls of one of the most remarkable church buildings I know of in the world, St. Lawrence Church in Lohja, Finland (or Lojo, as it is called in Swedish), there exists an extensive set of early sixteenth-century wall paintings that surround the assembly that meets there with biblical and liturgical images interpreting what happens in the meeting. Among those images are two that especially strike me as important to the identity of that assembly and all assemblies. Painted at the rear of the room as if embracing the gathered congregation, the risen Christ, carrying his cross, is leading a whole group of naked people out of the mouth of death and hell. And in another place, near the entrance to the church, a woman—Mary, perhaps, or Ecclesia personified or both—is sheltering a similar group of naked people under her great cloak. To practice a spirituality of the assembly is to know that we who gather are naked, needy people who are being pulled out of death by Jesus Christ and are together able to shelter under the covering cloak of ekklesia/assembly.

But not just shelter. Having been so pulled out of death and so covered, we turn to our neighbors and a needy world. The assembly in God's mercy so forms us. Another striking church building I know is a thatched mud hut in a village in Cameroon. There is nothing on its walls except one wooden cross above the simple table at the front of the room, a room that is otherwise filled with low benches for the assembly. But on the day when I saw this room, a blackboard for literacy lessons stood on that table. A table for the Bread of God and a table for words that help people to learn, succeed, and live in the world: such good uses for the assembly's table, such a good sign of the Sending.

Part Two

A Critical Catechism for the Assembly

5

Catechism and Sacraments

The Purpose of Assembly

Baptism joins us to an assembly and so joins us to the communion of assemblies or, rather, echoing Paul, to the one assembly of God throughout the earth. Baptism also gives us several common, assembly-shared inheritances: the Bible, the shape of the liturgy, the sacraments, the treasury of Christian hymnody, and the classic texts of the Christian faith. Classic texts? These include the Lord's Prayer and the Creed, of course. But they also include the Ten Commandments and perhaps some passages from the Scriptures that can stand for the sacraments or that are regarded as basic to the sacraments. In Lutheran circles, these texts together are called the "catechism."

Among Christians generally, the word *catechism* can stand for an accessible manual of the faith or a set of questions and answers that intend to teach the faith. But whatever way the word is used, the classic texts that belong to all Christians will be under consideration in such a manual. Among some Christians, other things have also been included in catechisms: lists of virtues, of the deadly sins, and of the gifts of the Holy Spirit and also perhaps the Beatitudes from Matthew and the angelic greeting to Mary from Luke. But for our purposes, let us especially consider the Commandments, the Creed, the Lord's Prayer, and texts relating to the sacraments. All of these come as shared possessions to those who are baptized. They belong to all Christians. And read critically—that is, with critical biblical studies and history in mind—they can be seen as further keys to the purpose and meaning of assembly.

Baptism and Catechism

There is a history to the association of these texts with baptism. The Creed developed from the questions, drawn from Matthew 28:19, used in many early Christian baptisms and often accompanying a triple immersion. The candidate was asked, "Do you believe in the Father? Do you believe in the Son? Do you believe in the Holy Spirit?" Slowly a baptismal "symbol"—a text that expressed baptismal faith—developed out of these questions and their expected responses. That text was then seen as what one confessed when one came to be baptized and what the assembly confessed when it was remembering baptism. This baptismal symbol had different forms throughout the churches, though everywhere it followed the tripartite outline first proposed in Matthew 28 and first used in the baptismal questions. The so-called Apostles' Creed was a Western development from the old third- and fourth-century baptismal symbol used in Rome. When, in the fourth century, the Councils of Nicaea and of Constantinople undertook to elaborate orthodox Christian faith more extensively in what ultimately became the Nicene Creed, they began by editing and adding to an earlier baptismal Creed, probably one used in the church of either Jerusalem or Caesarea. The Creed then, in whatever form, originally belongs to baptism.

Now think of the other texts of this catechism. Candidates for baptism do not learn only the Creed. They also learn to pray, and for such learning, the prayer said to have been taught by Jesus and included in both Matthew and Luke is fundamental. People coming to be baptized also are asked if they are willing to change their manner of life, and for such inquiry, the "Ten Words," as they are called in the Hebrew Scriptures, can form one insightful basis. These candidates also are then brought to the water and, through the water, are brought to the table and to the ongoing life of forgiveness in the assembly. The fascinating thing about the order of the catechism as it was adopted by the Reformation in the early sixteenth century is that it can be seen to represent and thus recall the whole process of baptism: candidates or the parents and sponsors of candidates are asked the questions about life change (the *Ten Commandments*), candidates learn the faith (the

Creed), they learn to pray (the *Lord's Prayer*), and they are brought to *baptism* and through baptism to the *Lord's Supper* and to life together with other Christians.

Martin Luther argued that any Christian should be a lifelong student of this catechism, probing again and again what these texts—and thus the baptism for which they stand—mean for theology and for life. He himself said that even though he had a doctorate in theology, he wished to be a daily student of the catechism throughout his life. Luther wrote two manuals in which he reflected on these texts—the *Small Catechism*, with questions and answers especially for teaching in households, and the *Large Catechism*, consisting of essays that were probably originally sermons. But it was not these manuals that he proposed for this lifelong study. It was the texts themselves. Then in several passages of his *Large Catechism*, he seems to indicate the existential crisis to which such study can lead.

Here is how he describes this crisis, more or less: We read the Commandments, and we know that, if they are taken seriously, we cannot truly keep them. So aware of our failure, we turn to the gifts of God's grace to which the Creed testifies. But on our own, we simply cannot believe. So we try to pray and, there too, we fail—we do not know how to pray. But at last, in the assembly of the church, we are reminded that we are baptized! And in that same assembly, we are given the gift of Christ's body and blood. Then with our "evenchristians," we find that we can begin to pray. And as we are praying, the Holy Spirit leads us backward into the Creed, starting in the Third Article, the article about the Spirit and the church. Faith is given to us as a gift as we join in what the assembly confesses. Then confessing God's gifts of grace, we begin to find ways that we can indeed keep the Commandments as they are reinterpreted in the light of faith and of the needs of the present day. Luther's fascinating forward and backward reading of the catechism was one fruit of his constant study of the gift of these texts. So was his seriousness about the catechism, combined with his critical, reinterpretive use of its texts. So was his sense of always being a beginner, coming again and again to faith.

But then we need to notice that each of us is brought to remembering again that we are baptized *in the assembly*, that the eucharist is the *assembly's* regular practice, that we pray to "*our* Father" in and with the *assembly*, that the *assembly* confesses the Creed with each of us, and that the Commandments have proposals for our communal action.

What is important for us in a spirituality of the assembly is that every one of these texts—themselves an assembly inheritance—has something to say about assembly. Reading backward, starting thus with the sacraments, the remainder of this book will seek to find what it is that the catechism says about our subject, how the classic texts of Christianity make clear that assembly is an essential inheritance for the baptized. Such an inquiry can be part of our own lifelong study of the catechism.

In each case, we will begin with the symbolic text or texts that belong to us through baptism and that together can be seen as making up the catechism. The symbolic texts that may stand for the sacraments and the sacramental word include these:

> Go therefore and make disciples of all nations, baptizing them in the name of the Father and of the Son and of the Holy Spirit. (Matt 28:19)

> This is my body that is for you. Do this in remembrance of me. . . . This cup is the new covenant in my blood. Do this, as often as you drink it, in remembrance of me. (1 Cor 11:24–25)

> Truly I tell you, whatever you bind on earth will be bound in heaven, and whatever you loose on earth will be loosed in heaven. (Matt 18:18)

> When [Jesus] was at the table with them, he took bread, blessed and broke it, and gave it to them. Then their eyes were opened, and they recognized him; and he vanished from their sight. They said to each other, "Were not our hearts burning within us while he was talking to us on the road, while he was opening the scriptures to us?" (Luke 24:30–32)

Again: Baptism, Eucharist, and Assembly

We have already thought about how learning baptism and eucharist by heart means learning assembly by heart. But now we need to inquire of the catechism, How does what it has to say about the sacraments matter for the meaning of assembly?

The classic texts used in the catechism to stand for baptism and eucharist are the texts that have traditionally been taken to be the "institution narratives" of these two sacraments: the passage about mission at the end of Matthew (28:16–20) and the passage about the Lord's Supper in the Pauline critique of Corinthian Christian meal practice in 1 Corinthians (11:17–34). These texts are sometimes supplemented with parallel passages in the longer, probably not original ending of Mark (16:15–16) and in the passion narratives of all three Synoptic Gospels (Mark 14:22–25; Matt 26:26–29; Luke 22:14–20). Especially Matthew 28 and 1 Corinthians 11 stand for the sacraments in the catechism.

But we should note that the use of isolated verses as "proof texts" always runs great risks, even here. One needs to think about the context of these verses in larger works—in Paul's correspondence, in Matthew's whole Gospel book, and in all the Gospels—and one needs to continue to think historically and critically. Thus ascribing the actual beginning of baptism and eucharist to the historical Jesus is very likely not accurate. Passages like 1 Corinthians 10:1–4, in which the Christian practice of baptism and the sacred meal are compared to the Exodus account of the passage through the sea, the eating of the manna, and the drinking from the rock, do make it clear that Christian communities were enacting these sacraments by at least twenty or twenty-five years after Jesus's death. It is not at all clear, however, how either practice began. The Gospels, all together, seem to indicate that while the historical Jesus was baptized by John, he never baptized anyone himself (see John 4:2). Christian baptism, rather, is associated with the risen Christ. The disciples are encountering the risen One in Matthew 28, the very end of the Gospel book, and that account includes the clearest directive that Christians are to baptize. There is no earlier command to baptize in the story of Jesus. Then in 1 Corinthians 11, Paul is very likely speaking about an instruction he himself received from the risen Lord, not unlike other places in his correspondence where he reports such revelations (see, for example, Gal 1:12 and 1 Cor 14:37). The accounts of the Last Supper in the passion narratives of the Gospels, written between fifteen and thirty years after Paul, most likely depend in varying ways on what Paul wrote, not on anyone's memory. The Lord's Supper also comes from the crucified and risen One.

But Christian baptism and the Lord's Supper, however they began, are best regarded as having come about by the reform and transformation of earlier practices: an eschatological washing and communal meals now used in Christian assemblies, at least at the instruction of Paul and of the Gospel writers, to proclaim and encounter Jesus Christ. Now the washing to be ready for the day of the Lord—as practiced by John the Baptist and perhaps by some very early followers of Jesus—has become washing into Christ, into his death and resurrection and the Spirit poured out from him. The assembly of those baptized has been made into a community of witnesses to God's mercy in these last days. Baptism founds that assembly. And now the communal meals of the Christian movement are being made into the assembly's encounter, in the power of that same Spirit, with the presence, identity, and life of Jesus, with his encounterable body and his life-giving blood. The communal Meal has become a foretaste of the final banquet, an eating and drinking now with God, and a necessary turning toward a hungry and needy world. Such a constantly reformed Meal has become the weekly Sunday practice of Christian assemblies.

But then we need to say more about "eschatology." It is clear that Christianity arose in a time when people formed by the Scripture were earnestly expecting the last days, the coming of the "day of the Lord." Paul speaks about this expectation in his letters, and the Gospels present Jesus as proclaiming the near approach of God's manifest reign. But the amazing insight of the Christian faith was the trust that, against all expectation, the crucifixion of Jesus Christ was already the hidden beginning of that reign and that the risen Christ, present in the assemblies, was and is the "first fruits" of the day of the Lord. The Spirit of God poured out in assembly from the death and resurrection of Jesus is the Spirit of the last times already now. In the late first century, the Letter to the Hebrews urged Christians not to neglect to meet together "and all the more as you see the Day approaching" (10:25). Thus the assembly was—and is—an explicit turning toward that Day. Indeed, the assembly was—and is—a means to see the Day, its meaning, and its presence already now.

The theological weight of the idea of "institution" can be important to Christian faith if it calls attention to the trust that baptism and eucharist do speak and enact Jesus Christ. Indeed, the faith of the church is that baptism and eucharist both correspond to his crucified and risen identity as that identity is present in the Christian assembly. The verses that are used for the sacraments in the catechism can, if read carefully, function as symbols for baptism and eucharist, making it clear that these practices come from the risen Christ and thus from the Spirit in the life of the assemblies. Taken critically and carefully, these symbolic verses—the texts about the sacraments in the catechism—are thus important to the assembly meaning for which we are looking.

So the text that can symbolize baptism is this: "Go therefore and make disciples of all nations, baptizing them in the name of the Father and of the Son and of the Holy Spirit" (Matt 28:19). This sentence speaks to a plural "you." The mission is not given to an individual; a community of disciples is sent. A larger community of the baptized is then expected. The "name" in which baptism is to take place throughout all the nations recalls the Matthean account of the baptism of Jesus: the assembly of the baptized will be given the same Spirit that was poured out on Jesus in his baptism, and those baptized will be gathered into the life of this triune God. Teaching is to occur, conjoined with baptism, the very teaching with which the Gospel book is full—that book is given to the assemblies as a handbook for their teaching. Then the risen Christ promises, "I am with you always, to the end of the age" (Matt 28:20). The "you" in this promise is again, of course, plural: it is the assembly. This assembly has a center—the presence of the risen Christ—and the assembly has an eschatological role "to the end of the age."

Similarly, the catechism text that can be seen as standing for the Lord's Supper includes these words: "This is my body that is for you. Do this in remembrance of me. . . . This cup is the new covenant in my blood. Do this, as often as you drink it, in remembrance of me" (1 Cor 11:24–25). Again, the "you" is plural. And that plural group is directed to "do this." The Lord's Supper is practiced by the assembly. Speaking then to the meal-keeping assembly, Paul adds this promise, "For as often as you eat this bread and drink the cup, you proclaim the Lord's death until he comes" (1 Cor 11:26). Again, the community—the assembly, the *ekklesia*—has an eschatological role.

In these two sacraments, much of the purpose of the Christian assembly can be seen. In the face of all the fears that can attach to the rather regular human expectation of the end of the world—including our own fears fueled by disease, war, climate change, and poverty—the assembly is to teach, baptize, proclaim, and gather people into the merciful identity of the triune God known in the presence of the crucified and risen Christ. It is to set out the means whereby fears of all sorts can be transformed into faith and hope and love. The most important ingredients of any end of the world are already present: God's promise, God's forgiveness, God's presence. The assembly bears this witness.

The Keys

We can also see the assembly meaning and purpose in two other sacramental realities that are set out in the New Testament. One of these also has a place in the catechism—it is called "the Office of the Keys." The biblical text that can stand for this practice is this passage from the Gospel according to Matthew: "Truly I tell you, whatever you bind on earth will be bound in heaven, and whatever you loose on earth will be loosed in heaven" (18:18).

This same promise is made to Peter after his confession, and there this authority to bind and loose is called "the keys of the kingdom of heaven" (Matt 16:19). But the passage in chapter 18 takes place in the midst of a discussion of sin and reconciliation in the assembly—the one place in the Gospels where the word *ekklesia* is used—and is addressed again to the plural "you" of that assembly. Envisioned here we find the mutual responsibility for forgiveness in the assembly. And once again, as with the texts about baptism and the eucharist that we have seen in the catechism, the practice is anchored in the presence of the risen Lord in the assembly: "Where two or three are gathered in my name, I am there among them" (Matt 18:20). Authoritative forgiveness is also an assembly practice.

Of course, individual Christians are urged to practice forgiveness, as, for example, in Mark 11:25: "Whenever you stand praying, forgive, if you have anything against anyone." And Peter's keys are also rightly exercised publicly in the assembly and individually for the assembly by persons ordained to do that apostolic ministry among us. But here, the assembly itself, even when it is only made up of two or three, is charged with enacting forgiveness. John's Gospel seems to put this Matthean charge and its connection to the presence of the risen One into a narrative account. According to John 20, on the first day of the week, the risen Lord comes among the assembled disciples, shows his hands and side, speaks the peace, breathes on the assembly, and says, "Receive the Holy Spirit. If you forgive the sins of any, they are forgiven them; if you retain the sins of any, they are retained" (20:22–23).

Based on such texts, Dietrich Bonhoeffer, in *Life Together*, argued that Christians should hear one another's confessions of sins and speak God's word of absolution—that any Christian might do this, such absolution being not only the province of the ordained. Bonhoeffer, as he sketched a rule of life for the students in his Nazi-resisting seminary, regarded such a practice between fellow believers to be representative of the whole assembly: "In the one other Christian to whom I confess my sins and by whom my sins are declared forgiven, I meet the whole congregation. Community with the whole congregation is given to me in the community which I experience with this one other believer. For here it is not a matter of acting according to one's own orders and authority, but according to the command of Jesus Christ, which is intended for the whole congregation, on whose behalf the individual is called merely to carry it out."

Whether or not our community encourages such a community-based practice of "private" or individual confession and absolution between fellow believers—or, to say it in another way with Luther, a practice of "the mutual conversation and consolation of brothers and sisters" (*Smalcald Articles* III:4)—we can say that the New Testament vision is that forgiveness, in many different ways, will be a steady mark of the Christian assembly. We enact forgiveness in all the ways we return to the font: at the beginning of a Sunday liturgy, in participating in someone else's baptism, in the reconciling practices of Maundy Thursday, in the baptismal renewal of the great Vigil of Easter, and when a sponsor helps a child to remember baptism. Our presider proclaims forgiveness standing at the font in the liturgy. Furthermore, preaching the gospel includes not simply talking about forgiveness but actually forgiving. The reconciliation of the sign of peace proclaims forgiveness. The Lord's Supper proclaims forgiveness. None of this involves a mild indulgence of sin. The Keys also lock or bind. Forgiveness in the assembly takes sin seriously: the assembly is a gathering of sinners, and the repeated proclamation of forgiveness acknowledges that great need.

As we will see when we consider the Lord's Prayer, God's forgiveness was expected to be fully present in the world only at the Day of the Lord. Then, also in the exercise of the Keys, the assembly anticipates that Day. The presence of the risen Lord in the assembly and the presence of the Spirit enable yet another purpose for the assembly: the manifest presence of God's eschatological forgiveness in the world now by its regular, enacted use there.

And the Sacramental Word

There is yet another purpose for the assembly: the presence of God's living word, the Word that can, again and again, bring us to faith. This Word especially comes to expression in the second part of the assembly's *ordo* that we have considered above, but it is also present throughout the Sunday meeting: in prayers and hymns, in gathering and dismissal, and in the promises associated with the sacraments. The word of God is "sacramental" in the assembly because of the trust that Christ is encountered as present in its utterance. While such a presence is assumed everywhere in the teaching of the church, this sacramental Word does not actually have its own place in the historic catechism. Were we to choose a catechism text to symbolize the sacramental Word, it might be the passage at the end of the Gospel according to John that intends to indicate the purpose of the Gospel book: "Now Jesus did many other signs in the presence of his disciples, which are not written in this book. But these are written so that you may come to believe that Jesus is the Messiah, the Son of God, and that through believing you may have life in his name" (John 20:30–31). Or it might instead be the passage from the Emmaus account at the end of the Gospel according to Luke: "When [Jesus] was at the table with them, he took bread, blessed and broke it, and gave it to them. Then their eyes were opened, and they recognized him; and he vanished from their sight. They said to each other, 'Were not our hearts burning within us while he was talking to us on the road, while he was opening the scriptures to us?'" (Luke 24:30–32).

Both of these texts demonstrate a purpose for the Gospel books we have already considered: all four of the books themselves intend to enact the presence of the risen Christ in the assembly. Reading carefully, we come to understand that Mark's Gospel, which lacks a resurrection appearance at the end of the book, is itself a resurrection appearance whenever it is read. The conclusion of the book sends us back into the book to see the risen One there, hidden in the story but manifest now in the assembly. The center of the book, which is made especially significant by the circular structure of the whole, is a house assembly in Galilee (Mark 9:30–50). There the risen One is shown to be present in all such assemblies where the story of the passion is told, where the leaders serve, and where the least and littlest are welcomed.

The other Gospel books use Mark, but they indicate the presence of the risen One in differing ways. Matthew, as we have seen, shows that presence in the reconciling assembly, enacting the keys (Matt 18:20), and in the baptizing and teaching assembly indicated at the end of the book (28:20). Luke knows that the risen One comes to serve in a Meal assembly where the leadership should likewise serve (Luke 12:37; 22:27). But Luke also knows that Christ is present when all the Scriptures, not only the Gospel book, are interpreted in the assembly (24:27). And John finds the risen Christ in the assembly, Sunday meeting after Sunday meeting (John 20:19, 26), where the Gospel book does indeed show forth his signs and bring us to faith.

Also, the Scripture in assembly—and the faithful preaching of the Scripture in assembly—enacts a sacramental presence. The ecumenical three-year lectionaries are precisely intended to so open the Scriptures that this sacramental presence is seen and heard. So John 20 and Luke 24 also help us see again the purpose of the assembly. In word and sacrament, by the power of the Spirit, we gather around matters that bring Jesus Christ to expression—indeed around the risen Christ himself—and so we gather before the face of God. We are brought again to faith.

In the assembly, against all fears and failure, we learn again that we are baptized. In the assembly, we are fed with mercy and forgiven. In the assembly, the Scriptures are opened to us. So as lifelong students of the catechism, we begin again to read backward through the classic texts that are given to us in baptism, reading this time to see the role of the assembly. It is no wonder that the assembly should be called "the fundamental sacrament of the risen Christ."

* * *

In the Danish National Museum in Copenhagen, there hangs a painted wooden altar frontal that originally hung in the village church in Torslunde, not far from Copenhagen. I am deeply grateful to have been able to see that painting and to be able sometimes to use it in teaching. Painted in 1561, it was meant to represent the Sunday liturgy as it would take place in any assembly that took Reformation principles seriously. At first glance, the scene seems chaotic: there are many people, some standing, some kneeling, some seated on the ground. There seem to be several clerics, but they are all vested differently—in black robe, in black robe and surplice, or in alb and chasuble. On one side, a baptism is taking place. On the other side, a preacher holding a Bible is in a pulpit with hearers gathered before him. In front of the altar, a man and a woman are receiving communion. All the central events of the assembly are taking place at once, and the assembly itself seems like a great crowd.

But as one looks, the disorder is drawn into order. There is a crucifix on the altar, like that crucifix in the church of my youth where I was an acolyte. And sight lines run out from the crucifix to the rest of the painting, creating a unity. The crowded assembly has room for us to come as well. And its practices have a center in the cross of Christ. By the power of the Spirit, that death makes the communal use of the Scripture the life-giving word of God, the communal taste of the Meal the taste of the resurrection also for us now, and the communal bathing the continual entry into this open assembly of witness for the needy world. In spite of the differences of culture—of clothing, of gender roles, of posture, even of vestments—this at first seemingly disorganized picture can speak to us. Our assemblies are called to the same central things. Our doors need to be open to the crowd. We are easily as disordered. And our unity—our purpose, our sacraments—is rooted in that same cross.

It is likely that the Torslunde frontal stands in a tradition of painted images of assembly around word and sacrament that began with Lucas Cranach's 1547 altarpiece in St. Mary's Church in Wittenberg. There too the image of what the congregation does is set out in front of the congregation. There too the congregation looks like a crowd, seeming to indicate room also for us. And there too the crucifix centers the whole—like that crucifix in my youth that held together the sorrows and the hopes of the people in the room. Interestingly, however, the Wittenberg altarpiece is divided into separate scenes: Jesus Christ presides in an image of the Last Supper while both the ancient disciples and also current figures—including Luther—are gathered with him; Philip Melanchthon is baptizing a child; Martin Bugenhagen, the principle pastor of St. Mary's Church, is hearing confession and exercising the Keys; and, beneath all of this, Luther is preaching to an assembly of real people from the time, an assembly that spills over the edge of the painting. Luther holds a Bible, but the content of the preaching is indicated by the crucifix to which he points, standing in the midst of the painted room. That crucifix functions also as the cross on the top of the Table of the eucharist, itself just below this painting. And that crucified Jesus in the image is clothed with a white loincloth that improbably billows out from the body in both directions in a room where there would be no wind. So the Spirit is poured out from the crucified and risen Christ, enlivening the preaching, consecrating the holy Meal, bringing the assembly to faith, and making the crowd to be God's assembly.

These sixteenth-century painted images are a kind of catechism. They are, as Joseph Leo Koerner says, pictures of the acts and objects that make church visible. More, they are pictures of the assembly of God occurring, taking place. They show the purpose of assembly. They pull us in, include us. And they make clear that sacraments and preaching both essentially involve assembly.

6

The Lord's Prayer

Assembly, Bread, and Forgiveness Now

The symbolic text for prayer is,

> Our Father in heaven,
>   hallowed be your name,
>   your kingdom come,
>   your will be done, on earth as in heaven.
> Give us today our daily bread.
> Forgive us our sins as we forgive those who sin against us.
> Save us from the time of trial
>   and deliver us from evil.
> For the kingdom, the power, and the glory are yours,
>   now and forever. Amen.

Then we begin to pray. The symbol for our praying is the prayer that the Gospels say Jesus taught, the prayer that forms our next catechism text. Considered carefully and critically, this text also speaks to us of the assembly.

Such consideration includes critical biblical studies. In a healthy spirituality of the assembly, it will be important to note that these critical studies are not destructive; on the contrary, used responsibly, they can serve a grace-full, realistic, mature, and orthodox faith. They can anchor that faith in an honest reading of the Bible. In the case of the Lord's Prayer, these studies help us see what might have been the context of the two forms of the prayer in the New Testament, what might be the oldest form of the prayer, what the prayer may have originally meant, and what it can mean for us today.

Both Matthew and Luke give us texts of the prayer, differing slightly and presented in different contexts. In Matthew (6:9–11), the prayer occurs in the Sermon on the Mount, in a section devoted to unique Christian practices in almsgiving, prayer, and fasting—practices especially marked by simplicity and an absence of display. In Luke (11:2–4), the prayer is presented as the answer Jesus gives to the request of a disciple: "Lord, teach us to pray, as John taught his disciples" (11:1). In both cases, then, the prayer is seen as an identifying characteristic of the movement around Jesus. And in both cases, the prayer is taught to a community: "teach *us* to pray," says the disciple in Luke; "*our* Father" prays the Matthean text. Already in these references, we begin to encounter the assembly and its identity.

It is likely that the prayer predated the Gospel books and that the differing forms presented in Matthew and Luke represent texts that were in use in the assemblies known by the authors of those books—for Matthew, most likely communities of Jewish-Christians and, for Luke, most likely Gentile assemblies. The differences in the texts can be seen to correspond to those contexts—"our Father in heaven" being an elegant old Jewish prayer phrase; "debts" being a possible way to talk about sin in the Jewish context, since in Aramaic "debt" could be a metaphor for sin; and the briefer rhetoric of Luke being especially useful in Gentile mission. Perhaps the text does indeed go back to the historical Jesus. We will see that the theology of this prayer can be understood to correspond rather closely to what can be said of the preaching of Jesus. On the other hand, perhaps the prayer originated with a Christian prophet speaking in the name of the risen Lord early in the movement that became Christianity after the death of Jesus. In any case, most scholars now think that the original text of the prayer would have been in Aramaic—the language of Jesus, the most common language of Palestine at the time of the origin of Christianity, and the language of the earliest forms of the movement that became Christianity. That Aramaic background is important as we think about the prayer's meaning.

One reconstruction of what might have been the earliest form of the prayer, translated into modern English, reads like this:

> Father,
> sanctified be your name, your kingdom come.
> Our bread for tomorrow, give us today;
> Forgive us our debts as we herewith forgive our debtors;
> and do not bring us to the test.

On the other hand, the longer and rhetorically richer Matthean form is the prayer that has been widely adopted in the churches. It occurs among us now usually with a doxology added at the end, a doxology already found in a late first-century or early second-century book called the *Didache* and also in some Greek manuscripts of Matthew. The current ecumenical version of the prayer, as adopted by the English Language Liturgical Consultation and widely used in the churches, is the one printed at the outset of this chapter. With both texts in front of us, let us think about what this catechism symbol shows us about assembly.

The Lord's Prayer as an Eschatological Text

We have already seen that the early meanings of baptism and eucharist demonstrate that the assemblies were invited to see themselves as communities of the last times, as places where "the Day" could begin to be seen, as places for the "foretaste of the feast to come." The same idea is present in the Lord's Prayer. It is fascinating to note that one of the oldest prayers of the Jewish synagogue that still exists is the prayer called the *Kaddish*. This prayer is important for us in recovering the eschatological sense of the Lord's Prayer. The *Kaddish* takes several slightly differing forms in current synagogue life: the prayer that the reader of Scripture in the *qahal* chants when he or she has finished reading or that is prayed at several other places in synagogue liturgy; the prayer that is chanted when part of the Talmud or Mishnah has been read; the prayer at the original end of a synagogue service; and, probably most widely known and beloved, the prayer prayed by a mourner. All these forms contain something like these lines:

> Exalted and hallowed be his great name
> > in the world which he created according to his will.
> May he establish his kingdom during your lifetime and during your days
> > and in the lifetime of the whole house of Israel, speedily and soon.
> And say, Amen.

One form includes these final lines:

> May the prayers and supplications of all Israel
> be accepted by their Father who is in heaven.
> And say, Amen.

The *Kaddish* is prayed in Aramaic in the synagogue, not Hebrew. One theory is that it began as a prayer recited by synagogue preachers or teachers at the conclusion of their preaching or teaching and that it then used the same vernacular Aramaic that had been used in the sermon or discourse, Aramaic being the most widely used language among Jews in the first centuries of our era and the same vernacular that marked the beginning of the Christian movement. This prayer was begging God for the fulfillment of the biblical promises that the preacher or teacher had just been interpreting. The *Kaddish* thus is an eschatological prayer, a prayer for the great Day to come. It is no wonder that in the Middle Ages it began to be used to commemorate the dead; in the face of death, the faithful Jewish community prays for God's reign to come, God's life-giving Day to dawn. What is more, among Orthodox Jews a *minyan*—at least ten men—is required for the *Kaddish* to be publicly prayed. In the synagogue, this praying for the Day belongs to an assembly.

The Lord's Prayer also prays for that Day. And though the Christian sense of what is needed for an assembly differs, the Lord's Prayer also belongs to the assembly. A comparison between the Lord's Prayer and the *Kaddish* makes clear the similar eschatological character of the prayer attributed to Jesus. "Hallowed be your name" and "your kingdom come" are phrases that occur also in the *Kaddish*, albeit in the Lord's Prayer they are directly addressed to

God. They both mean essentially the same thing: "We beg you, O God, in a time of great need, let your reign of justice come, bring the healing of harms, gather your people into life. Act so as to make your name holy, so that all over the world people will praise your name." Then the petition that Matthew's Gospel adds—"your will be done, on earth as in heaven," an idea at which the *Kaddish* hints—also means the same thing: "as all the universe does your will, come, we ask you, O God, and do your will here; bring the Day of your manifest will." In those passive verbs—"be hallowed" and "be done"—God's own action is hidden and hoped for. At least in its first three petitions, the Lord's Prayer breathes the same atmosphere as the *Kaddish*. Indeed, it most likely arose around the same time and was formed out of the same motifs of prayer. If the prayer does come from the historical Jesus, it is quite possible that he already knew and used the *Kaddish*.

There are differences between the prayers, of course. The Christian prayer addresses God directly. It does not make use of the third person masculine pronoun, which seems to be a respectful way to avoid using God's name. A phrase that in the *Kaddish* only occurs toward the end of the longer form—"Father in heaven"—has become the opening address in the Christian prayer. And while the Christian prayer most likely began in Aramaic, as with all Christian worship it now takes place in the many local vernaculars: Christianity is a translation religion, and Christian assembly is always seriously local, also in language.

There are at least two other important differences. One is that in the eschatology of the Lord's Prayer, the old promise of the coming Day included a sense that a time of great difficulty, of testing to see whether the assembly would remain faithful to God, would precede this coming. The Christian prayer begs to be saved from such testing. Christians should honestly acknowledge that they are not strong—they are needy sinners—and cannot easily think they would pass the test. More, Christians believed that the Day of God had already begun to dawn in Christ and that he himself had faced the time of testing for us all: his cross was that dreadful time, and the story of his "temptation" in the wilderness turned such testing into a narrative. But whether or not Christians will be saved from a time of trial, the prayer in Matthew's form begs God simply to deliver us from evil—or, perhaps, remembering the story of Jesus in the wilderness, from the evil one.

This reflection on the eschatological setting of the sixth and seventh petitions of the prayer makes clear one important reason the earlier common translation of the Lord's Prayer—"lead us not into temptation"—is so wrong and should be abandoned. God tempts no one, as both the letter of James (1:13) and Martin Luther (*Small Catechism*) fiercely argue. Rather, what is imagined is the great eschatological testing, the testing that Christians believe Jesus has already faced and that they humbly admit they might not be able to survive.

But there is another important difference between the *Kaddish* and the Lord's Prayer: surrounded by these prayers that the Day will come and that the community may survive the test, bread and forgiveness are mentioned. And with these two, we come even more seriously to the current Christian assembly.

The Ecclesiology of the Lord's Prayer

It may seem odd to talk about the Lord's Prayer having an ecclesiology—teaching about what the *ekklesia*, the assembly, the church itself is—but in truth, the prayer does at least imply such teaching. We have sensed that earlier in noting that the Gospels show the prayer as being taught as an identifying characteristic of the disciples of Jesus, as being the prayer of his community. We also see it in those first-person plurals: *our* Father, give *us*, forgive *us*, save *us*, deliver *us*. In the Lord's Prayer, however, the community of Jesus's disciples is praying petitions that belong to all humanity. Everyone needs such bread, forgiveness, and deliverance, and here the community is praying—like a company of priests for the sake of the world—for everyone. The first thing to say about the *ekklesia* in the Lord's Prayer is that it willingly takes up that task. If it is a specific, identified group, it builds no walls around that identity. It prays, it works—it exists!—for the sake of the life of the world. The Day is coming and has already dawned for all the world, and the Christian assembly prays that it may come with mercy and hope for everyone.

The "trial" and "deliverance" petitions also exhibit an ecclesiology. This company of priests for the sake of the world ought to know itself as weak, themselves in need of God's mercy and strength. So Martin Luther wrote in the note found by his own deathbed the last words we had from him: "I say we are beggars. This is true."

But there is more. Surrounded by petitions that, like the *Kaddish*, are manifestly marked by a hope for the last Day and by petitions that know that that Day will come also with danger and threat, the assembly speaks of bread and forgiveness. The importance of these themes is underscored by the Gospels themselves. Immediately after the text of the Lord's Prayer in Matthew, there follows a reflection—a sort of footnote or excursus—on forgiveness (6:14–15). Immediately after the text of the prayer in Luke, there follows an excursus on asking for bread (11:5–13), "bread" being here—as in the prayer itself—a synecdoche for all food.

But bread and forgiveness also belong to the eschatological themes of the prayer. We have already seen that the earliest Christians expected the final feast—the feast against death described, for example, in Isaiah (25:6–9)—as a central event of God's Day. They also thought that in the present dawning of that Day, the eucharist in the church already participates in that feast. But forgiveness, too, belongs in God's future. "The days are surely coming, says the Lord, when . . . I will forgive their iniquity, and remember their sin no more," wrote Jeremiah in the important passage about the new covenant (Jer 31:31, 34). It is probably the idea that true forgiveness from God is waiting for the last Day that stood behind the grumbling about Jesus forgiving people: "Who can forgive sins but God alone?" (Mark 2:7).

In the Lord's Prayer, bread and forgiveness are now, here, in the assembly. The word translated "daily" in the bread petition is a unique word; *epiousian* occurs nowhere else in Greek. It could mean something like "bread for existence." But imagining the Aramaic original of the Lord's Prayer, scholars have proposed that the Aramaic word here very likely meant "tomorrow." So the petition was "our bread for tomorrow, give us today, we pray." The "tomorrow," then, was the hoped-for Day itself, the bread a "foretaste of the feast to come," as one liturgical canticle has it. The Gospels tell the stories of Jesus eating with sinners with the sense that they are being included in the coming reign of God already now simply by eating with him. The Gospels tell of Jesus feeding the multitude as if this were already Isaiah's feast. The Gospels tell of the risen One coming to serve his followers at table. The Gospels, with Paul, tell of Jesus interpreting his own death at a meal where he gives himself away. The Gospels tell of the crucified risen One eating and drinking and showing himself alive. All of these meals are presented as the Day of God already dawning. And the Lord's Prayer belongs with all these meals.

That does not mean that the bread petition has nothing to do with our actual daily meals. On the contrary. For Christians, the eucharist is our Meal *par excellence*. But all of our other meals circle around and echo the eucharist. "Come, Lord Jesus, be our guest," we pray with the disciples at Emmaus, "and let these gifts to us be blessed. Blessed be God, who is our bread. May all the world be clothed and fed." For Christians, aware of the dawning Day, every meal is a meal with God and needs to be marked by the thanksgiving and hospitality that belong to Christian life. Recently, during the pandemic, when holding eucharist in the assembly was not possible, we needed to remember that joy in the ordinary again. Unable to gather at the eucharist, we could find the risen Christ nonetheless making holy our own tables in our own lives, turning us toward the hungry poor of the pandemic time.

But in the assembly—in the eucharist in the assembly—we come to the central way in which, Sunday after Sunday, by the mercy of God and the gift of the Spirit, we may trust that the bread petition is being answered.

So is the forgiveness petition. Because of Jesus Christ and the breathed-out Holy Spirit (see John 20:22–23), the forgiveness of the end is already present now in the assembly. It is not that we are forgiven to the extent that we forgive. Rather, we celebrate the presence of the forgiveness of God now by also now—herewith, in the prayer, and from our hearts—forgiving people who have sinned against us. But the amazing thing is that God's forgiveness, "the Keys," are here, in the assembly, now.

The ecclesiology of the Lord's Prayer is this: This assembly stands with the world, praying for the needy, knowing itself to be needy. It does not distinguish itself from the world. Rather, it identifies with the world and does so especially in its longing and urgent prayer. But at the heart of its life, by the merciful gift of God, because of the death and resurrection of Jesus Christ and through his outpoured Spirit, the bread and forgiveness of the end-times are already here. The Lord's Prayer expresses both things: the assembly waits and prays with the whole world, and yet it receives the signs of the grace and life for which it prays. The assembly is the community given this prayer—taught it at baptism, repeating it at every eucharist. The assembly tells the truth about the world's need and joins all humanity in longing. In bread and forgiveness, the assembly celebrates already now the presence of God's healing of harms. It is then sent into the world to forgive and to share food with the hungry so that the daily meals and the personal interactions of Christians might echo and extend the assembly.

The Theology of the Lord's Prayer

But these things are true of the assembly because of the theology to which the Lord's Prayer bears witness, the very theology that is at the heart of the assembly. What is that theology?

Some commentators on the prayer have taken its theological uniqueness to be located in the first word of the Lukan form: "Father." Scholars have thought that this simple address might stand for the Aramaic word *Abba,* a word that could represent a strikingly intimate name for a father—something like "papa." The word occurs three times in the New Testament, twice in Paul (Gal 4:6 and Rom 8:15) and once in Mark (14:36). Paul uses it to argue that the Spirit motivates Christian prayer as witness to the person praying being a child of God and a coheir with Christ. Mark has this same prayer address on Jesus's lips when he is alone in Gethsemane. It may indeed be the case that this form of address to God was beloved by early Christians. It may also be that they regarded that its use came from the historical Jesus. But proposing that it evidences a uniquely Christian language and a uniquely Christian intimacy with God is probably saying too much. *Abba* in Aramaic can be read simply as a vocative form of the word for father; it can mean simply "O, father" or "listen, father." And we have seen that

"Father in heaven" was already a name for God in the longer form of the *Kaddish*. "Father" was also quite present in Greco-Roman religion: Zeus was called *Zeus-pater* or "Jupiter" in Roman temples. "Father" as address for God is not unique to Christianity. Indeed, "Father" as a Christian word carries a lot of difficult, potentially sexist baggage and is in need of being criticized, nuanced, and saved. Several decades of Christian thought recently have been dedicated to that task.

As part of that "saving," we should recognize that the real uniqueness of the Lord's Prayer—related to its understanding of the assembly—is its subtle trinitarian character. In the prayer, God the Father is the one to whom we pray, before whom all humanity is full of both longing and fear. But God is also the one who, in Jesus, has come to be with humanity in its longing, need, fear, and death. Since Jesus is regarded as the one who teaches us this prayer, the prayer itself can be seen as an extension of his presence. He prays with us, or we pray in him. The articulation of human need and fear in the prayer is a concrete sign of God's coming among us, all the way into needy death. Furthermore, God is the one who—in the resurrection of Jesus poured out into the assembly through the presence of the Spirit—has begun to give us both forgiveness and bread as a first taste of the healing of all harms. The Spirit enables those gifts and thus enlivens the assembly.

The uniqueness of the Lord's Prayer is found in the assembly having the articulation of need from and together with Jesus and having, at the same time, the presence of bread and forgiveness—thus the trinitarian heart of the prayer. This God is not three gods but one life-giving God. Such trinitarian theology can be seen as manifest in the three reference points of the prayer, all enfolded in the divine unity and in the assembly gathered into that unity: the Father to whom we pray; Jesus, who teaches this eschatological prayer of need and prays with us; and the Spirit, who prays in us and makes bread and forgiveness alive at the heart of the assembly.

Some liturgies have rightly brought this theology to expression by this introduction to the communal praying of the Lord's Prayer: "Gathered into one by the Holy Spirit, let us pray as Jesus taught us. Our Father in heaven, hallowed be your name . . ." The assembly is gathered into one in the Spirit. The assembly has learned to pray from Jesus. The assembly stands before the Father.

Whether or not the use of *Abba* comes from Jesus, it is true that the prayer can be seen to represent much of what we presume about the preaching and ministry of the historical Jesus. It certainly can be seen to represent Jesus as he is presented in the Gospels. The address to God as Father can be found in several Gospel passages, as, for example, Matthew 11:25 ("I thank you, Father, Lord of heaven and earth . . .") or the Johannine version of the Gethsemane prayer in John 12:27 ("Now my soul is troubled. And what should I say—'Father save me from this hour'? No . . .").

The petitions for the coming of the reign of God correspond to Mark 1:14–15: "Now after John was arrested, Jesus came to Galilee, proclaiming the good news of God, and saying, 'The time is fulfilled, and the kingdom of God has come near; repent, and believe in the good news.'" The petition about bread corresponds to the many meals of Jesus, seen as signs of the advent of God's reign: "This fellow welcomes sinners and eats with them" (Luke 15:2). The petition about forgiveness corresponds to Jesus enacting forgiveness: "When Jesus saw their faith, he said to the paralytic, 'Son, your sins are forgiven.' Now some of the scribes were sitting there, questioning in their hearts, 'Why does this fellow speak in this way? It is blasphemy! Who can forgive sins but God alone?'" (Mark 2:5–7). And the petitions about the test and the evil one correspond to the narratives of the testing of Jesus in the wilderness: "He was in the wilderness forty days, tempted [read *tested*, the classic meaning of *peirazomenos*] by Satan" (Mark 1:13). They correspond also to the accounts of the crucifixion in the Gospels, Jesus's most serious and awful "test": "Aha! You who would destroy the temple and build it in three days, save yourself, and come down from the cross!" (Mark 15:29–30).

While the prayer is addressed to the Father, it is full of the Jesus of the Gospels. It is also full of the Holy Spirit. It is fascinating that a few ancient manuscripts of Luke and a few old teachers have in their texts of the prayer—instead of "your kingdom come" (Luke 11:2)—this petition: "your Holy Spirit come upon us and cleanse us." That is doubtless not the original wording. Still, it illuminates two matters: First, the coming of the Spirit was also regarded as gift of the end-times, a gift that the Lukan narrative of Pentecost or the Johannine account of the risen Christ breathing the Spirit onto the Sunday assembly celebrates as already being given. And second, the ability to pray to the Father and the very presence of bread and forgiveness are rightly seen as signs of the Spirit.

The Lord's Prayer—taught at baptism, received as one of our symbolic texts, repeated at every eucharist, prayed as a daily prayer—enacts how the Christian assembly is gathered into the very life of the triune God. That gathering will, of course, also be the confession of the next symbolic text, the Creed.

* * *

I join with many others today in loving the classic icon of the holy Trinity painted—or, as they say, written—in the early fifteenth century by the Russian Orthodox icon maker Andrei Rublev. Based on the classic story from Genesis 18 about the three angels (visiting "men" in the text and yet also, in the men, the visiting Lord God) eating with Abraham and Sarah and promising them a child, the icon shows the three gathered at a table. Nothing else except a tree—the "oak of Mamre"—and a fragment of a building is shown. The three form a gracious circle around a cup in the center of the table. In the cup, barely visible unless you look closely, is a lamb. One of the three—intended to represent the Son of God—raises his hand to bless the cup as if also to assent to being that lamb. All three figures bend toward one another in a gentle dance of love. One almost sees them moving. And there is room at the table. The side of the table toward the viewer is open; the viewer is being invited to come to that cup in the midst of the represented Trinity.

Bread and forgiveness in the assembly are like that cup. We come to them, drink, are forgiven, forgive, encounter the Lamb of God, feel the breath of the Spirit, bow toward the Father, and are gathered into the life of the triune God. The Lord's Prayer can be read as words for that icon, or the icon can be seen as the Prayer made into an image.

More, bread and forgiveness are like the gold, white robes and sight-giving salve offered to the assembly at Laodicea (Rev 3:14–23). With that assembly, we ought to know ourselves to be "wretched, pitiable, poor, blind, and naked" (Rev 3:17). But the risen One stands at the door of the assembly, knocking. In bread and forgiveness, he comes in, giving us that cup, gathering us to sit down with his Father. And that is what the Spirit is saying to the churches.

One more thing: when we can gather again safely, in care for the health of our communities and our neighbors, the Lord's Prayer helps us see how important the assembly is. The author of the letter to the Hebrews wrote, "Let us consider how to provoke one another to love and good deeds, not neglecting to meet together, as is the habit of some, but encouraging one another, and all the more as you see the Day approaching" (Heb 10:24–25). The Lord's Prayer, read as an eschatological and trinitarian text, is such encouragement. And the third-century author of the *Didascalia* wrote, "Since you are Christ's members, do not scatter yourselves from the church by failing to assemble. . . . Do not, then, neglect yourselves; do not deprive our Savior of his members; do not rend and scatter his body. . . . On the Lord's Day leave everything and hasten to the church. Otherwise, what excuse before God have those who do not come together on the Lord's Day in order to hear the word of life and to be nourished with the divine food that remains forever" (II:59).

We can hear the scolding voice of that old third-century bishop. Perhaps the scolding will not help us—though the appeal not to "deprive our Savior of his members" is moving. But the word of life and the divine food on the Lord's Day, bread and forgiveness now, will draw us: the cup in the midst of the Trinity, salve to anoint our eyes so that we may see.

7

The Creed

Assembly and the Communion of Saints

The symbolic text of the Creed, in its two forms, is,

> I believe in God, the Father almighty,
>   creator of heaven and earth.
> I believe in Jesus Christ, God's only Son, our Lord,
>   who was conceived by the Holy Spirit,
>   born of the virgin Mary,
>   suffered under Pontius Pilate,
>   was crucified, died, and was buried;
>   he descended to the dead.
>   On the third day he rose again;
>   he ascended into heaven,
>   he is seated at the right hand of the Father,
>   and he will come to judge the living and the dead.
> I believe in the Holy Spirit,
>   the holy catholic church, the communion of saints,
>   the forgiveness of sins,
>   the resurrection of the body,
>   and the life everlasting. Amen.

* * *

> We believe in one God,
>   the Father, the Almighty,
>   maker of heaven and earth,
>   of all that is, seen and unseen.

> We believe in one Lord, Jesus Christ,
>> the only Son of God,
>> eternally begotten of the Father,
>> God from God, Light from Light,
>> true God from true God,
>> begotten, not made,
>> of one Being with the Father;
>> through him all things were made.
>> For us and for our salvation
>> he came down from heaven,
>> was incarnate of the Holy Spirit and the virgin Mary
>> and became truly human.
>> For our sake he was crucified under Pontius Pilate;
>> he suffered death and was buried.
>> On the third day he rose again
>> in accordance with the scriptures;
>> he ascended into heaven
>> and is seated at the right hand of the Father.
>> He will come again in glory to judge the living and the dead,
>> and his kingdom will have no end.
> We believe in the Holy Spirit, the Lord, the giver of life,
>> who proceeds from the Father [and the Son],
>> who with the Father and the Son is worshiped and glorified,
>> who has spoken through the prophets.
>> We believe in one holy catholic and apostolic church.
>> We acknowledge one baptism for the forgiveness of sins.
>> We look for the resurrection of the dead,
>> and the life of the world to come. Amen.

The sacraments in the assembly and the sacramental word have reminded us that we are baptized. They have drawn us again and again into the mercy of God. Then we have begun again to learn how to pray. Praying, we have found ourselves speaking for all needy humanity, including ourselves. And yet we have been taken as an assembly into the very life of the holy Trinity. We have come to the cup of the lamb, to the bread and forgiveness of the end-times already present now. And we have been called to let those central marks of the assembly show in our daily lives: sharing food and sharing forgiveness. At least, such a movement through the experience of the catechism might be one way to construe the recurring shape of our Christian life.

Then we may be ready to confess the Creed. And in this book, we are ready to inquire whether the Creed also has something to say about the assembly.

This symbolic text, along with the other assembly-marking symbols, belongs to us through baptism. As we have seen, both historic creeds of the Christian churches have been shaped by the name in which we were baptized—that is, by Matthew 28:19—and by the history of the confession of that name. But the symbolic text of the creeds also needs to be received critically. For one thing, in its use, the Creed ought not be regarded as a password that lets you into a club or a means of excluding some people. It ought not function as a *shibboleth* (see Judg 12:6), shutting out people who cannot quite say it. Used in the Sunday liturgy, it may sometimes feel like that is its purpose. Furthermore, especially the Nicene Creed uses Greek philosophical concepts and Greek rhetoric in ways that make the text difficult for many of us in the present time. It is no wonder that current liturgical commentators sometimes urge that the classic Christian faith may come to clearer expression in the Sunday assembly in other ways: in responsible preaching, in fine new hymnody, in intercessions, and in eucharistic praying, for example. Indeed, as some current rubrics allow, the Creed can rightly be regarded as optional in the eucharistic liturgy.

But the Creed is also a gift. Read carefully, we can regard it as a treasured historic text that links us to Christians through the ages—as a sign of communion through time. The Nicene Creed invites us to confess that "we believe . . ." It is a communal symbol, an assembly-based confession of the faith, not an individual examination. That any individual Christian might not put the matter just this way in the present time can coexist with the community together setting out this historic symbolic language.

Still, the Creed of the Western catechism is not the Nicene Creed but the Creed of baptism, the Apostles' Creed. That text summarizes in a simpler way the classic questions and responses of baptism. Although, in some communities, this Creed too may be used in the Sunday eucharist, its primary home is in baptism—in preparation for baptism, in the baptismal rite itself, and in occasions for the renewal and affirmation of baptism. If, among us, the Nicene Creed may stand as a symbol of communion with generations of Christians, the Apostles' Creed stands as a symbol of what was given us in those life-giving waters.

Two matters here need to be accentuated: the creeds are *symbols*, and they are *communal symbols*, used by the assembly. At the very outset of this book, we thought about the assembly itself as a basic, essential symbol of Christianity. That assembly then also uses further symbols, and the creeds are among them. Thus, like any symbol, they are meeting places. They gather us together to encounter a larger meaning, in this case to encounter the faith of the church for which the creeds stand. When we confess such a symbol, we symbolically enact that faith, and we enact it together. It is not that we "believe in" the Creed. It is that we believe in God—that is, we find ourselves together invited to trust in God, and the Creed gives an outline of that trust, being as we use it one expression of that trust. And there are two of them! One set of words is not enough. In fact, this doubling, representing as it does both the West (the Apostles' Creed) and the East (the Nicene Creed) in Christianity, undercuts any idea that our faith is in the Creed. Rather, surrounded by this double witness, we are invited to trust in God. But we use only one at any given time. Though there are two, the function in the flow of the catechism and in the liturgy is singular, so—while remembering that doubling—we will continue here to speak of "the Creed."

WE BELIEVE

The first way we encounter assembly when we encounter the Creed is in that plural. A community makes this confession of faith, and that community understands itself to be in communion with all the assemblies where this text has lived. Indeed, the Creed is one of the instruments of that communion between assemblies. The original form of the Creed adopted in the fourth and fifth centuries at Nicaea, Constantinople, and Chalcedon—and called the Nicene Creed—used that first-person plural. The Latin-speaking church changed the plural to the singular, imitating the form of its baptismal Creed. More recently, and rightly, Western churches have been recovering the plural of the Nicene Creed in their vernacular liturgies. The orthodox faith organized into these three paragraphs is a faith that belongs to an assembly in communion with other assemblies, all together making up the "we."

Even the "I believe" of the Western baptismal Creed has an assembly basis. The baptism occurs in assembly and joins an individual to the assembly. The individual being baptized, along with those who are bringing that individual to the water, takes on the assembly's faith. Each one inserts their own "I" into the assembly's Creed. When the Creed is confessed at baptism, most commonly, everybody joins in. That Creed has been taught in assembly—confessed at baptismal occasions and sometimes at the eucharist in assembly—and becomes one symbolic means of the individual being grafted into the living thing that is assembly.

And the assembly carries the responsibility, in communal dialogue, to keep on interpreting what this symbol means. The faith it expresses is not a dead set of unchangeable concepts but a living trust in the triune God who comes to expression in many ways in the assembly's life: in Scripture reading, in preaching, in the sacraments, in teaching, in hymn singing, in mutual conversation and consolation, in "Christ existing as assembly," in care for the world and especially the poor, and even in images on the walls of the house of the church. All of those things juxtaposed to the articles of the Creed call for an ever-renewed interpretation. Interpretation, not replacement: the historic texts are themselves the symbols. We do not rewrite them. We receive them, live with them, interpret them. Theologians, preachers, hymn writers, and every individual Christian in dialogue with the assembly of Christians and in communion with all the assemblies through history carry that reinterpreting responsibility.

Martin Luther undertook such fresh interpretation in the sixteenth century in his *Small Catechism* with its simple, profound, and existential summaries of the three parts of the Creed: "I believe that God has created me together with all that exists"; "I believe that Jesus Christ, true God . . . and also true human being . . . is my Lord"; and "I believe that by my own understanding and strength I cannot believe in Jesus Christ my Lord or come to him, but instead the Holy Spirit has called me through the gospel . . . just as [the Holy Spirit] calls, gathers, enlightens, and makes holy the whole Christian church on earth." These summaries are, of course, glosses on that "I believe" of the Apostles' Creed. Creation, redemption, and the call to faith and to ecclesial life are all things that happen to "me"; they are not distant, abstract events. The first paradigm of creation faith is trust in what God is doing to us now, not speculation about some ancient divine act. Similarly, for Luther, the paradigms for redemption and for sanctification by the Spirit are found in that "my Lord" and that "called me." Still, Luther's explanations do not only focus on individuals. The *Small Catechism* is intended to be a book of the assembly and of the assembly as it is echoed in the home. It is a book for teaching in community. Every "I" is a treasured part of that personal, communal assembly.

The reinterpretation goes on. Thus *The Pastor*, the companion book to this one, expressed one such reinterpretation of the Creed for the twenty-first century in this way:

> The Christian church teaches us to trust that God is creator of this actual, material world; God has made and still cares for all that is. In a world that largely thinks of spiritual truths as being unconnected with the material, inviting us out of here, that confession is already an astonishing assertion, a daring trust. But there is more. Far from God being distant from a world full of suffering, in this same church I am invited to trust Jesus Christ. The church teaches us to trust with our lives that God, in Christ, has shared our human life, sorrows and death, saving all things and all of us together for forgiveness and life. I am invited to trust that God's own heart, God's very own self, who God actually *is*, is encountered in the man Jesus, and that because of the resurrection we may indeed so encounter this Jesus Christ here in the meeting of the church as well as in all of those suffering

ones with whom he identifies. But there is yet more. The assembly of the church itself, as it stands before the creator of all in company with the words and signs of this Jesus, believes it is enlivened by the very presence of God, called the Holy Spirit. Only so, may we come to the astonishing trust called *faith*. Yet, having said all of that, it is important to add that there are not three gods, but one God. Indeed, for Christians, this account of the Spirit enlivening the meeting so that, in a suffering world, we may gather with the risen One before the face of the source of all things—this trinitarian account—is what makes the trust in one God possible at all. When I was baptized I was gathered into a community that trusts these things: the actual world is good and held by God; this same God engages with the real suffering, sin and death of all this world, and may be encountered where we had not expected God to be; and this same God gives us the gift to live out of such faith rather than out of fear and guilt and death. I was brought through the waters to trust that there is a good creation, that I can tell the truth about suffering and death, and that God's Spirit is life-giving.

And when I find that I cannot trust that confession—when my faith waivers—I can fall back on the sense that others in the community are making the confession for me. The Creed is an assembly symbol. We believe together.

Backward into the Creed

Moving backward through the catechism with Luther, we start into the Creed with its third article. As Luther says, "By my own understanding and strength I cannot believe in Jesus Christ my Lord or come to him, but instead the Holy Spirit has called me through the gospel." Such a confession shows the believer only coming to the second and then the first article—to trust in Jesus Christ present amid the world's great need and trust in the One who creates all good—by first encountering the Spirit. In coming to faith, by this view, we come first to the Holy Spirit and to the assembly: "I believe in the Holy Spirit, the holy catholic church, the communion of saints, the forgiveness of sins, the resurrection of the body, and the life everlasting." Thus the second and most important way we encounter the assembly in the Creed comes to expression here. The assembly—the church, the assemblies in communion with all the assemblies, the catholic church (that is, the believing church found all over the world)—needs to be mentioned when we discuss the Christian trust in the Spirit. Indeed, as we have found again and again in thinking about assembly here, if the assembly is faithful, it is enlivened by the Spirit.

But there are a lot of spirits in the world. We say, "It was a spirited meeting" or "The spirit in the room was not healthy" or "There is a sweet spirit in this place" or "They had a lot of spirit." But when is the spirit in a room the Holy Spirit? When is it the presence of God?

The Gospel according to John (3:8) says that the Spirit of God goes where it wills, blows like a wind in ways beyond our control. This is true, but nonetheless, Christians, while controlling nothing of God, have largely followed Paul's word about the Spirit: "I want you to understand that no one speaking by the Spirit of God ever says 'Let Jesus be cursed!' and no one can say 'Jesus is Lord' except by the Holy Spirit" (1 Cor 12:3). The final great discourse in the Gospel according to John (in chapters 13–17) has similar Christological criteria for understanding the presence of the Spirit: "[Jesus speaks:] '. . . the Advocate, the Holy Spirit, whom the Father will send in my name, will teach you everything, and remind you of all that I have said to you. . . . When the Advocate comes, whom I will send to you from the Father, the Spirit of truth who comes from the Father, he will testify on my behalf. . . . When the Spirit of truth comes, he . . . will glorify me, because he will take what is mine and declare it to you'" (John 14:26; 15:26; 16:13–14). The Spirit in the room bears witness to Jesus Christ, crucified and risen, if it is the Holy Spirit. If it is the Holy Spirit, we will be led to trust Christ as Lord, and we will be brought to trust the One who made all things good.

Christians have believed that the Spirit that enlivens an assembly in the gospel, an assembly around Christ in word and sacrament, is the same Spirit of which the New Testament narrative repeatedly speaks: the Spirit that overshadowed Mary at the incarnation (Luke 1:35; Matt 1:18), that was poured out on Christ at his baptism (Mark 1:10), that was given by Christ for the thirsty to drink (John 7:37–39), that was given over by Jesus in his death (John 19:30, 34), that the risen Christ breathed onto the assembly of disciples when sending them to forgive (John 20:22), or that descended on the assembly at Pentecost (Acts 2:1–13). Indeed, for Christians, that Spirit is also the same Spirit that swept over the waters in the first creation story (Gen 1:2), that gifted Bezalel with wisdom to craft the Tabernacle (Exod 31:3), that came upon the prophets in Israel (1 Sam 10:10), that Isaiah promised for Jesse's descendent (Isa 11:2), that Ezekiel saw making the dead bones live (Ezek 37:10), or that Joel promised for the last days (Joel 2:28–29). By that Spirit, our assemblies too are made to live, like dry bones standing up; our assemblies too will know the Spirit that rested on the shoot from the stump of Jesse; our preachers too will speak the word of God; our assemblies will be, like the Tabernacle, a dwelling place of God; and our gathering too will be drawn into the new creation. Our assemblies will be already living in the last days. An assembly where the gospel of Jesus Christ, the gospel of the mercy of God for the life of the world, is sung, preached, read, eaten, drunk, and lavishly poured in water over the bodies of those baptized is, quite simply, an assembly in the Spirit.

Some people may indeed experience this Spirit with an abundance of emotion, a kind of religious ecstasy, or other charismatic gifts. Many others may not. Christians have many different kinds of personalities. Such emotion and such gifts can be profound and personally important but unfortunately can also mislead. Strong emotion is not the criterion for the presence of the Spirit; the gospel of Jesus Christ is, as Paul argues so clearly in 1 Corinthians 12. The Spirit of God may be anywhere, surprising us with hope and life. But a primary place where we may encounter that gospel and its enlivening Spirit is in the assembly, enacted communally, spoken to us by the assembly's presider and its other ministers, always coming to each one of us from outside of ourselves.

The Communion of Saints, the Participation in Holy Things

Two phrases in the article of the Creed about the Spirit further identify the assembly, and those phrases are in apposition. That is, the noun phrases are intended to say the same thing in different terms, functioning as explanatory equivalents of each other. Those phrases are "the holy catholic church" and "the communion of saints."

We have already seen how second-century Christians—as in the assembly of Christians in Smyrna writing about the death of Polycarp—could speak of the faithful assemblies as "the holy catholic church sojourning in every place" (*Martyrdom of Polycarp*, initial inscription). An assembly in a given place makes it possible to encounter "the catholic church" to the extent that this assembly abides in and is continually reformed by the gospel of Jesus Christ, doing so in communion with the other assemblies. Such an assembly, as we have seen, is the holy catholic church—that is, the church made up of faithful churches found throughout the world—dwelling in a particular place and set apart (which is the meaning of "holy") to bear witness to God's mercy for the life of the world.

But the Creed says yet more. This assembly, which is the holy catholic church dwelling here, can also be spoken of as "the communion of saints." On first reading, this phrase speaks of the *communio*—the *koinonia*, the fellowship, the communion, the shared life—of a holy people. Who are these "holy people"? Paul and many of the New Testament authors after Paul use the term *saints* to speak of the present participants in the assemblies (see Rom 1:7; 1 Cor 1:2; 2 Cor 1:1; Phil 1:1; etc.). They are made holy in Jesus Christ. They are called to be holy as they are called by God to participate in the assembly of God. Making a meeting to be the assembly of God, the symbol of God's people bearing witness to God's mercy for the life of the world, makes that meeting—that assembly—to be "holy church." This "holiness" is not in the first place a manifest moral virtue. Rather, "holiness" here speaks of God's action in identifying these people to be "priests" for the sake of the world. Again, to be "holy" means to be set apart to that purpose, for the life of the world, not for themselves. Then those holy people are in shared life with one another. Baptized, they devote "themselves to the apostles' teaching and fellowship [*koinonia*], to the breaking of bread and the prayers" (Acts 2:42). Besides prayer and the eucharist and the apostolic preaching of the gospel, they themselves are given to one another. Dietrich Bonhoeffer was right when, anticipating the long loneliness of his own resistance to Nazism and his own imprisonment, he wrote, "The physical presence of other Christians is a source of incomparable joy and strength to the believer," and, quoting Luther's interpretation of Psalm 109, that such presence is a rare gift, the "roses and lilies" of the Christian life.

We should recall that this was the same Bonhoeffer who warned against any attempted immediacy in relationship that seeks to circumvent the mediation of Christ in the shared symbols. We come closest to one another in those symbols. In the sign of peace, we begin to see Christ greeting us in the other. Around the holy cup, we begin to be formed to be with one another as those angels are with one another in Rublev's icon of the Trinity. Our communion with one another—our "fellowship," thus (see 1 John 1:3, 7)— begins to be like the very communion that is in God and to be founded on communion with that triune God.

In assembly, we are invited to learn deep respect and empathy for each of the others. What happens to any of the others happens to all of us. If someone is baptized, all of us are back at the one baptism that has received us all. If anyone is in grief, it belongs to us all. If anyone is in joy, that is a common gift. Of course, this does not always happen among us. Churches are also places of brokenness and the misuse of others. But we are called to be holy. We are given one another in the communion of saints. More, just as we pray in the Lord's Prayer the petitions that belong to all of needy humanity, the signs of mutual respect and care for one another we learn in the assembly direct our care and respect toward all the world, toward every other creature around us, toward the earth itself. The *koinonia* of holy people in the assembly is not that of an exclusive club; it is a training ground for walking in the world.

Such a use of the word *saint*, of course, differs from our ordinary current use. We usually use the word today to mean a dead person of unusual moral or spiritual distinction—even a dead person whom one or another church has specifically designated as a "saint." That is not entirely wrong. As the assemblies lived into more decades and then more centuries after the origin of Christianity, a deep trust grew that the *koinonia* of the *ekklesia* was not broken by death. The shared life of the people of God includes the grateful remembrance of those who have borne their witness in many ways and have now died in Christ. Already the seer John of the Apocalypse sees those who have been slain for the faith as "saints" (Rev 5:8–9). Some of those we know; some—a great "cloud of witnesses," as the letter to the Hebrews says (12:1)—we do not. The annual celebration of All Saints Day and the recurring commemorations of various Christians throughout the world and throughout the ages give us ways to exercise such a grateful remembrance, including its surprise at the many different (and even odd) kinds of witness to God's mercy there have been.

But the primary meaning of "the holy people" remains the current members of the assembly being given that shared life.

There is, however, something more to say about assembly and the *sanctorum communio*, as the Latin phrase of the Creed has it. *Sanctorum* can indeed mean "of the holy people." It can also mean "of the *holy things*." The plural noun can be both masculine, standing for people, and also neuter, standing for things. The same would be true if the phrase were in Greek: *koinonia tōn hagiōn*. So the phrase in apposition to "the holy catholic church" might be translated as "the shared participation in the holy things."

It seems best to regard the Creed as meaning both at the same time: the holy people and the holy things. The holy catholic church enlivened by the Spirit and dwelling in a specific place is an assembly of shared life—a communion of people God is making holy, making into witnesses of mercy. At the same time, this communion is an assembly of shared participation in the holy things of God, the things that bear God's grace for the life of the world: the Scriptures, the gospel, baptism, the holy supper, mission and outreach, and in all of this, "the forgiveness of sins." One can read the two phrases *sanctorum communio* and—following it in Latin—*remissionem peccatorum*, the forgiveness of sins, as also being in apposition, functioning as explanatory equivalents of each other. The phrases then move on in a progression of appositional meaning: the catholic church here in assembly, that church as the very shared participation in the holy things, and the holy things as summed up in the forgiveness of sins. The forgiveness of sins in the assembly, so important to the meaning of the Lord's Prayer, can stand for all the holy things in which the assembly shares and that, indeed, constitute and ground the assembly of God: bread and forgiveness.

In some places in the New Testament, *koinonia*—for which *communio* may stand in the Latin and *communion* may serve in English—does indeed mean simply "fellowship," shared life with one another, in this case between "the holy people." The use of "fellowship" in Acts 2:42 and in 1 John 1:7 presents the primary examples of that meaning. However, the much more common meaning of the word in the New Testament is "participation" or sharing in something. Paul, using *koinonia*, speaks of himself sharing in the sufferings of Christ (Phil 3:10) and of Philemon sharing in faith (Phlm 6). But even more relevantly and still using *koinonia*, he speaks of communities or assemblies of Christians participating in Christ (1 Cor 1:9), in the Holy Spirit (2 Cor 13:13), in the body and blood of Christ (1 Cor 10:16), and in service to the poor (2 Cor 8:4). This latter list seems like the very list of "holy things" to which the Creed may well be pointing as it defines the "holy catholic church." Led by the Spirit, the church is a real assembly of people, given fellowship with one another by the love of God. At the same time, the church is a communal participation in the central matters of the meeting's mission, all these things being filled with the forgiveness of sins.

This very participation in the *koinonia* then promises life. The Creed calls this "the resurrection of the body, and the life everlasting," as the chain of phrases moves on. One should be careful not to deal with this promise as if it were an American movie about life after death. For Christians, "eternal life"—that is, real life—is in Jesus Christ and exists already now (1 John 5:11–13). And the respected bodies of the gathered assembly, signs of the respect due all creatures, are already signs that this life is not simply a "spiritual" idea. More we cannot say. The Creed simply invites us to trust God's promise, finding that promise reaffirmed in the holy assembly, in the fellowship of those who bear witness to God's mercy in the world, in the shared participation in the holy things of Jesus Christ who is the life, and in the signed forgiveness of sins.

Then the Nicene Creed says something like the same thing by calling the church "one holy catholic and apostolic," thus pointing to all the characteristics of the assemblies that we believe God is creating among us through the unity-making *koinonia* and the assembly-grounding apostolic gospel. Note that these characteristics cannot function as marks for us to find the church. The church—and each of our assemblies—is often actually disunited, refusing its holy mission, narrowly parochial and focused on itself, and lacking in the gospel, the preaching of the gospel that came to us from the apostles being what is meant by "apostolic." Rather, naming each of these characteristics is an act of faith; we believe that God is making the churches one, holy, catholic, and apostolic. This phrase is then followed by the Nicene Creed's way of pointing to the holy things that are at work among us and in our assemblies: "We acknowledge one baptism for the forgiveness of sins."

Two other phrases in the Nicene Creed need to be noted. Here the Holy Spirit is "the Lord," a title that bears witness to the Spirit being God but also a title that is usually applied in the New Testament to the risen Christ. By using this title, the Nicene Creed helps us see that the Spirit poured out in the assembly is the very Spirit that bears witness to this risen One. And the Nicene Creed says that the Spirit "proceeds from the Father." The phrase "and the Son" (*filioque* in Latin) was added later in the Western church, is offensive still to Eastern Christians, and probably should be dropped in the West on the same grounds of respect for the historical text that have been moving some churches to recover the "we believe." For this reason, the ecumenically received text of the Nicene Creed printed at the head of this chapter puts those words in brackets. Still, the texts we have quoted above from the Gospel according to John (John 14:26; 15:26) make clear that in the New Testament, the Spirit can be seen as both sent by the Father in the name of Christ and sent by Christ "from the Father." What the Spirit enlivens in the assembly—what the Spirit bears witness to—is much more important than this old debate over the *filioque*.

So we note that the Creed has a great deal to say about assembly. With the "we believe," with the Holy Spirit as the spirit of the meeting and the grounds in which participants in that meeting come to faith, with the caring fellowship, and with the shared participation in the holy things at the center of that fellowship, the Creed makes a signal contribution to a spirituality of the assembly.

* * *

In his Apology of the Augsburg Confession *(VII and VIII:20), Philip Melanchthon says plainly that the church ought not be seen as an ideal but unreal thing, invisible like the city of Plato's republic or purely "spiritual." Rather, it really exists—or it occurs, it takes place—and the marks whereby it can be seen occurring as a real assembly of real people are the gospel and the sacraments. Luther, for whom the marks were variously and more extensively summarized but included—as we have seen—the preaching of the gospel, baptism, eucharist, absolution, ordained ministry, prayer, and "the holy possession of the cross," also wrote, "Without place and body, there is no church."*

The "communion of saints" and the "shared participation in holy things" give us place and body and invite us again and again into those marks. While a house for the church—a building—can be wonderful, if we ask what we need in order to have church, the deep answer appears in those marks. Church happens in places where the assembly practices the marks, trusting that the Holy Spirit will use them in witness to God's mercy for us and for all.

The "communion of saints," the fellowship of those called to be holy, also gives a way to turn toward the world. Robert Hovda, the Roman Catholic liturgist from whom I have learned so much, used to bow as deeply to the congregation at mass as he did to the altar, perhaps more deeply. We can learn from such a bow as we deal with one another in the assembly but also as we deal with one another in the world. Whether we physically bow or not, we may bow in our hearts before the mystery of each other person. Or before the mystery of everything in the world.

In a remarkable passage in Arctic Dreams, *the foundational work by the recently mourned nature writer Barry Lopez, he writes about bowing to birds in their nests and to the landscape under arctic light:*

"I took to bowing on these evening walks. I would bow slightly with my hands in my pockets, toward the birds and the evidence of life in their nests—because of their fecundity, unexpected in this remote region, and because of the serene arctic light that came down over the land like breath, like breathing." Later, after mentioning phalaropes, oldsquaw, cormorants, auklets, whales, and seals, he writes, *"I looked out over the Bering Sea and brought my hands folded to the breast of my parka and bowed from the waist deeply toward the north, that great strait filled with life, the ice and the water. I held the bow to the pale sulphur sky at the northern rim of the earth. I held the bow until my back ached, and my mind was emptied of its categories and designs, its plans and speculations. I bowed before the simple evidence of the moment in my life in a tangible place on the earth that was beautiful." Formed in the* communio sanctorum, *Christians can learn from this account to recognize the profound gift of each tangible place, each tangible creature, beyond all our plans and designs, to whom we repeatedly turn in gratitude, empathy, compassion, and respect. Christians know the world is full of suffering. It is also, as the Creed confesses, good—and filled with beauty.*

8

The Commandments

Assembly, the Name of God, and the Neighbor

The symbolic texts for the Commandments are,

Exodus 20:1–3, 7, 8, 12, 13–17, 5–6

> Then God spoke all these words: I am the Lord your God, who brought you out of the land of Egypt, out of the house of slavery;
>> You shall have no other gods before me.
>> You shall not make wrongful use of the name of the Lord your God ...
>> Remember the sabbath day, and keep it holy ...
>> Honor your father and your mother ...
>> You shall not murder.
>> You shall not commit adultery.
>> You shall not steal.
>> You shall not bear false witness against your neighbor.
>> You shall not covet your neighbor's house;
>> You shall not covet your neighbor's wife, or male or female slave, or ox, or donkey, or anything that belongs to your neighbor. ...
> ... for I the Lord your God am a jealous God, punishing children for the iniquity of parents, to the third and the fourth generation of those who reject me, but showing steadfast love to the thousandth generation of those who love me and keep my commandments.

Matthew 22:35–40

> One of them, a lawyer, asked him a question to test him. "Teacher, which commandment in the law is the greatest?" [Jesus] said to him, "'You shall love the Lord your God with all your heart, and with all your soul, and with all your mind.' This is the greatest and first commandment. And a second is like it: 'You shall love your neighbor as yourself.' On these two commandments hang all the law and the prophets."

In the reverse consideration of the catechism, we have come last to the Commandments. We have already considered the sacraments, the Lord's Prayer, and the Creed, finding assembly important to all of them. But what about the Commandments? What do they have to do with assembly? The Lord's Prayer is repeatedly used in the liturgy of the assembly, and when read critically, it does have its own ecclesiology, its own important understanding of assembly. The Creed belongs in the baptismal process and may be used in the eucharist; in any case, it speaks clearly of the *ekklesia*. The texts that can stand for the sacraments have central use in the assembly's performance of those sacraments, sacraments that ground and center the assembly. But the Commandments? Except for the lectionary for the Third Sunday in Lent in Year B—and except for an occasional liturgical practice in some Anglican and Reformed churches—the Commandments are generally not heard in the Sunday assembly. It is at least initially hard to see how they relate to our project here.

Furthermore, except as a symbol for a conservative legalism, not uncommonly posted in churches or courtrooms in archaic speech, does anyone pay much attention to them anymore? They seem quite patriarchal, even hierarchical, coming so clearly from another cultural time and seemingly addressed only to free, land-owning males. Parents are to be honored, and that seems to bring along an insistence that all authority will be unquestioned. Slavery is taken for granted. It is the neighbor's wife—not her husband—that ought not be coveted, and in the form of the Commandments in Exodus, she is ranked along with the slaves and the domestic animals as property. Indeed, the prohibitions of "coveting" generally seem to imply that everybody ought to be content and keep their place in society.

But our commitment here has been to read the catechism critically, considering its contexts and reinterpreting it into our own times. Furthermore, the role of the Commandments in the baptismal process is to challenge us, to inquire of us whether we are willing to have our life and our values changed, reoriented away from current social values toward a life that reflects the mercy of God. Can a careful reading of the Commandments in our time make that challenge?

The remarkable thing is that the Ten Words, as they are called in the Hebrew tradition (see Exod 34:28; Deut 4:13; 10:4), have a long biblical history of lively reinterpretation. They have been dealt with as a living tradition of meaning, not a fixed and immutable text. The first such reinterpretation was simply their insertion into the exodus story, both in a priestly passage in the book of Exodus and in the book of Deuteronomy. A text from what was most likely an earlier, more simply phrased apodictic code was reunderstood as being ordained by the God who liberated the enslaved people of Israel: "I am the Lord your God, who brought you out of the land of Egypt, out of the house of slavery" (Exod 20:2). Liberation was seen to entail an ethics. And in one form of that insertion (Deut 5:15), the reason for the command of sabbath observance was taken to be a celebration of that very liberation, not a memorial of the seventh day of creation from Genesis 1 as in the Exodus version (Exod 20:7). Both reasons given for the sabbath are, of course, interpretations, and they are not the same. Then as time went on, both the Torah and the prophets engaged in constantly reunderstanding who the "neighbor" of the Commandments actually was.

In the Gospels, Jesus also reinterprets the Commandments. In Matthew's Sermon on the Mount, he makes them much harder: "You have heard that it was said to those of ancient times, 'You shall not murder. . . .' But I say to you that if you are angry with a brother or sister, you will be liable to judgment" (Matt 5:21–22); and "You have heard that it was said, 'You shall not commit adultery.' But I say to you that everyone who looks at a woman with lust has already committed adultery with her in his heart" (Matt 5:27–28).

Even more, all three Synoptic Gospels have a version of the narrative about the two great Commandments (Mark 12:28–34; Matt 22:36–40; Luke 10:25–28). In all these pericopes, whether Jesus or a lawyer whose words are approved by Jesus is the speaker, the Commandments are summed up by quoting part of the Shema about loving God (Deut 6:5) and then setting that magisterial and ritually important word next to a much more obscure part of the law about loving the neighbor (Lev 19:18). That this second is "like" the first is already a significant reinterpretation. That the two together anchor "all the law and the prophets" (Matt 22:40) or that they are "much more important than all whole burnt offerings and sacrifices" (Mark 12:33) makes the reinterpretation revolutionary. Then Luke appends to these two commandments a further understanding of who the neighbor is by telling the parable of the Good Samaritan (Luke 10:29–37): the one who shows mercy is neighbor to anyone who needs it, and in this case, the one who acts as neighbor is a despised outsider.

The Ten Commandments, of course, have been organized and numbered, and that organization itself involves a continuing interpretation. The listing above, at the head of this chapter, follows the Roman Catholic and Lutheran reading, in which "you shall not make for yourself an idol" (Exod 20:4) is regarded as an extension of the first commandment and the prohibition of the misuse of the divine name as the second commandment. Among both Lutherans and Roman Catholics, the prohibition of images has been largely set aside, the careful use of images being seen as important to Christianity. The Eastern Orthodox and Reformed reading, arising in two traditions that have been significantly marked by iconoclasm and its results, regards the prohibition of images as the second commandment. Furthermore, under the influence of the two great commandments in the Gospels, as associated with the Exodus narrative about "two tablets of stone" (Exod 34:4), Christians count two "tables" of the law, the first having to do with loving God, the second having to do with loving the neighbor. Lutherans and Roman Catholics, then, count three commandments in the first table and seven—including two prohibitions of coveting—in the second. Eastern and Reformed Christians count four and six, continuing to emphasize the prohibition of images as part of the four, though the Eastern and Reformed traditions deal with that prohibition in vastly different ways, ways that are also reinterpretations. People who publicly post the text of the Ten Commandments—or even simply post the Roman numerals I–X on two tablets—frequently do not realize that they are choosing one or another denominational tradition and that these traditions are not the same.

Reinterpretation of the Commandments has continued in the churches. Most Christians have dropped sabbath observance or massively reunderstood it. Some Christians have thought of a soldier's work as necessarily involving murder and have thus avoided armed service. Others have worked on theories of just war, arguing that a soldier too can be saved. Many Christians today think that authority of any kind can be rightly questioned or placed under critique. Slavery has come to be universally rejected by Christians. And a wife ought not be classed with property.

One of the most important works of Christian commandment reinterpretation can be found once again in Luther's *Small Catechism*. There, over and over, the prohibitions are turned into positive counsel. Instead of committing murder or doing other harm to our neighbors, we should "help and support them in all of life's needs." Instead of "bearing false witness"—telling lies and slander about our neighbors—"we are to come to their defense, speak well of them, and interpret everything they do in the best possible light." Some of Luther's reinterpretations may have worked especially well in sixteenth-century German society, such as the counsel against practicing magic or the urging that we not anger anyone in authority. But the modern pastor and teacher can take heart and learn from Luther's positive work here—the presence of wisdom, the absence of fundamentalism, the awareness that interpretation is indeed needed—when turning in our time to the important task of teaching the meaning of the Commandments and, more generally, teaching the shape of Christian ethics. Pastors and teachers need to see that this teaching task ought be addressed not only to children or confirmation classes but also, perhaps first of all, to thinking Christian adults.

But again, what about the assembly?

The Assembly and the Sabbath

One of the most consequential reinterpretations in Luther's explanations of the Commandments deals with the sabbath. That reinterpretation brings us again to the assembly.

When "What is this?" (*Was ist das?* in the German) is asked in response to "remember the sabbath day, and keep it holy" in the *Small Catechism*, Luther replies, "We are to fear and love God, so that we do not despise preaching or God's word, but instead keep that word holy and gladly hear and learn it." Suddenly the commandment is no longer about rest throughout a day in the week but about the gathering around the Word, read and preached, and thus about the assembly.

It may very well be that in our day, when work overwhelms many lives and true rest is hard to find—and when some computers or smartphones are never turned off—there is a new need to accentuate at least one day of rest in any week. Encouraging "sabbath" as a way to celebrate the goodness of creation and the goodness of the liberating God can be an important Christian theme, a theme Christians should gladly learn from the Jews. But it is simply not true that Christians in the early centuries made their meeting day into a new "sabbath." That idea arose in Puritanism in seventeenth-century England and in Reformed Christianity in seventeenth-century Scotland. The idea then became strong in nineteenth-century American Protestantism. But in the ancient world, Sunday was a workday, and even when the emperor Constantine in the fourth century made Sunday a day free from work in the cities, many occupations and virtually all farmers were exempted, and many of the poor could not afford such a break, in any case. No, from early in the Christian movement, the "Lord's Day" was not sabbath but was the day for the assembly to meet. Emeritus of North Africa reminds us that the thing he was willing to die for was that meeting, the Lord's Supper on the Lord's Day.

But then we may see the uniqueness of Luther's interpretation. While he does not name the assembly, he imagines hearing Scripture read and imagines preaching. Both take place in the assembly.

To understand how these relate to sabbath and rest, it is useful to read the argument in chapter 4 of the book of Hebrews as that writing interprets Psalm 95:7–11. The psalm sings out, "Oh, that today you would hear God's voice!" It warns that the ancient people of the exodus story tested God at Massah and Meribah even though, the narrative says, they had seen God's works. In response, according to the psalmist, God swore, "They shall never come to my rest." The book of Hebrews argues that the ancient people did not hear God's voice or did not hear and believe it: "The message they heard did not benefit them" (Heb 4:2). The author then draws the contrary implication that hearing God's word and trusting it—together hearing the "good news," the gospel of God (Heb 4:2)—bring a people into God's rest, enabling them to cease from their labors as God did in creation. "So then, a sabbath rest still remains for the people of God," the author writes (Heb 4:9). The immediately following praise of the word of God as "living and active, sharper than any two-edged sword" (4:12) makes it clear that this sabbath is not so much a day as it is the deep rest enabled by hearing the gospel, hearing "God's voice." Those phrases in Hebrews—"united by faith with those who listened" (4:2) and "the people of God" (4:9)—evoke the assembly as the place for such hearing of the living and active word. No wonder, then, that this same letter will later say, "Let us consider how to provoke one another to love and good deeds, not neglecting to meet together" (Heb 10:24–25) and, in images, "You have come to Mount Zion and to the city of the living God . . . and to the assembly of the firstborn" (12:22–23).

Luther, who would have regarded that everyone fails at the Commandments and everyone, like the ancient people at Massah and Meribah, tests God, found such rest in hearing the gospel. Thus his reworking of the sabbath commandment to point simply to hearing the word of God in assembly makes preeminent sense in his theology. For him, going to church to "gladly hear and learn" the word of God is the way to keep the commandment. His insight may be useful to us. Coming to deep rest may indeed involve a deep sense of forgiveness, an encounter with the thousandfold mercy of God. Hearing Jesus Christ say, "Come to me, all you that are weary and are carrying heavy burdens, and I will give you rest" (Matt 11:28) is one way to understand what hearing the gospel means. Christ is our rest, our sabbath. Only Christians ought not think this rest means passive inactivity. Rather, this rest is the lively rest of wisdom, the refreshed ability to turn in care toward the neighbor with the "love and good deeds" of which the author of Hebrews speaks, seeing that love and good deeds as encouraged by our meeting together.

For Christians, the sabbath commandment calls us to the assembly.

Assembly and the Name of God

So does the commandment concerning the name of God: "You shall not make wrongful use of the name of the Lord your God." Luther says, concerning this commandment, "We are to fear and love God, so that we do not curse, swear, practice magic, lie, or deceive using God's name, but instead use that very name in every time of need to call on, pray to, praise, and give thanks to God" (*Small Catechism*). Again, the prohibition is turned to positive counsel. An older translation of that positive counsel in the *Small Catechism* urged that we "call upon God's name in every trouble, pray, praise, and give thanks." While following this counsel can certainly be a personal or individual undertaking, calling upon God amid the world's trouble, praying, praising, and giving thanks are for Christians preeminently assembly activities.

Assembly, of course, also runs the danger of the "wrongful use of the name" of God. Religious lies and deception are certainly possible, and given the project of this book to think about assembly as a gift, they may appear to us as especially awful. The "prosperity gospel"—the promise that true believers will necessarily grow rich—or the personality cult of any preacher or healer are examples of such lies. So is rigid legalism or ritual fundamentalism or communal self-righteousness. These lies can destroy the assembly as a witness to the mercy of God for the life of the world. In many ways, religious lies in the assembly are worse than cursing, swearing, and practicing "magic." Still, we rightly see the commandment as encouraging the life-giving use of the name of God.

We should recall again the importance to any assembly of carefully crafted intercessions for real needs in the world. That is certainly one way we may regard the commandment as alive among us, one way we may faithfully use the name of God. But there are other prayers as well: a prayer when we assemble; a prayer before we depart; in some traditions, a prayer for illumination before the Scripture is read; a prayer at setting the table for the eucharist; and more. We should also recall that a primary action of the assembly is giving thanks, especially at the table of the eucharist and at the font. On analogy to the role of thanksgiving in the sacraments, a thanksgiving—or what is called a "prayer of blessing"—also proclaims the resurrection as the paschal candle is set out in the great Vigil of Easter or welcomes the light in Evening Prayer. Such a prayer is also used when a minister is ordained or when thanks is given for the marriage of a couple in a wedding rite.

All these prayers and thanksgivings are full of the name of God. And what is that name? One of the most significant developments in Christian liturgy in recent decades has been the increasing use of biblical images and metaphors to speak of God, to address God, and to bring to expression the Christian understanding of the triune identity of God. "Father, Son, and Holy Spirit" is certainly one set of such metaphors—a privileged set because of its role in baptism and in recalling baptism. But "Blessed be God, the source of all life, the word of salvation, the spirit of mercy," found in one baptismal rite sung in dialogue with the words from Matthew 28 that are used in the water, is also "the name of God." So also, at the holy table, is "O God most mighty, O God most merciful, O God our rock and our salvation," which does not mean to articulate separate characteristics of the three "persons" but to bring to expression the unfathomable richness in the triune God, a richness that includes both might and mercy. This concluding doxology of one recent eucharistic prayer celebrates that richness even more strongly:

> You, Holy God, Holy One, Holy Three,
> Our Life, our Mercy, our Might,
> Our Table, Our Food, Our Server,
> Our Rainbow, Our Ark, Our Dove,
> Our Sovereign, Our Water, Our Wine,
> Our Light, Our Treasure, Our Tree,
> Our Way, Our Truth, Our Life.

You, Holy God, Holy One, Holy Three!
Praise now, Praise tomorrow, Praise forever.

Contemporary hymnody also celebrates and sings the name of God. Consider this one stanza of the Easter hymn "Alleluia! Jesus Is Risen!" Here Jesus, the Spirit, and "heaven," as an image for God the eternal source, all are included in the name—a name that is coming toward us as gift, as fruit of the tree of life:

Jesus the vine, we are the branches;
life in the Spirit the fruit of the tree;
heaven to earth, Christ to the people,
gift of the future now flowing to me.

The "name of God" in current assembly practice has become a disciplined and trinitarian explosion of biblical images.

But the name of God is even more. As "name," it evokes the presence and the power of the one named and makes that one available to be encountered and known. As such, it does not only come to expression in hymns and prayers. Rather, the identity of God, the mystery of God made available to be encountered and known—even more, the mystery of God knowing *us*—can also be regarded as what is expressed by word and sacrament enacted in the assembly. The name of God is an assembly event. Several passages of Scripture, disciplined by the lectionary and read side by side in harmony and in tension with one another, express who God is. A good preacher continues that expression. The water in the font, used by an assembly together with Scripture, expresses who God is. Bread and wine together with thanksgiving and the word of promise, eaten and drunk in assembly, express who God is.

Christians have loved to borrow the words of Jeremiah to describe their understanding that the assembly meets now already in the new age: "No longer shall they teach one another, or say to each other, 'Know the Lord,' for they shall all know me, from the least of them to the greatest, says the Lord; for I will forgive their iniquity, and remember their sin no more" (Jer 31:34). Forgiveness in the assembly is the encounterable name of God, coming toward us now.

The name commandment, when it is read as positive encouragement, also points us toward assembly.

Assembly and the Neighbor

The remaining commandments are not so explicitly related to assembly, except that we have seen repeatedly in this book that faithful assembly practice turns us toward our "neighbor," toward the other human beings who live around us as well as toward all creatures in God's creation. The second table of the law—commandments four through ten in the Roman Catholic and Lutheran count and commandments five through ten in the Reformed and Orthodox numbering—can stand as symbols for that assembly-based turning. If the love of neighbor is "like" the love of God in the revolutionary proposal of the Synoptic Gospels, then we may see that both practices—letting the word of God in assembly bring us to lively rest and faithfully using the name of God in assembly—steadily open us to the reality, gifts, and needs of our neighbors. The first table of the law necessarily implies the second.

Recall what has been said in the reflections of this book: the focal practices of assembly, its song, and its metaphoric speech imply ways to see the world and to live in it. The intercessions and the thanksgiving send us to walk in prayer and in praise with our neighbors. Having learned and practiced mutual respect in the assembly, we may learn again a deep respect for all things, even bowing to the birds' nests or the whales. Different voices in the Scriptures, side by side, may help us imagine other points of view than our own and care about people who are different from ourselves. The Lord's Prayer causes us to stand with all who long for God's justice and to share bread and forgiveness. The eucharistic Meal may sensitize us to hunger and food insecurity in the world and may send us to be ourselves as bread for our neighbor. Eating and drinking the presence and life of Jesus Christ can awaken us to "fight, work, pray, and—if you cannot do more—have heartfelt sympathy" for the wretched of the world. The Sending of the liturgy—and the whole liturgy as a Sending—commissions us to make signs of love and service in the world around us. The assembly, when it faithfully gathers in word and sacrament, again and again gives us what we need to live in peace and to enact our own contributions to justice.

Of course, we will fail, also again and again. And the Commandments contain, in Exodus 20:5–6 and Deuteronomy 5:9–10, a warning to those who do not keep them, thus rejecting God: they will pass on to their children's children a spoiled world, marked by God's punishment. While that may not be how we would say the matter today, we do know the social and inherited consequences of our common sin. But the Commandments also promise a thousandfold social mercy—also extending to children's children, but for generations and generations—when even one person keeps a commandment. The rabbis did the math and were right to say that God's mercy is three to four hundred times greater than God's wrath. The assembly is intended to gather us around that mercy.

Coming from the sacraments to prayer, and then from prayer to the Creed, we may begin again to keep the Commandments. We may find our values indeed being challenged and changed. Brought to deep and lively sabbath rest, gathered around the name of God, we turn to our neighbors. It is not only that we must not kill, commit adultery, steal, bear false witness, or covet. It is even not only that, with Luther's positive counsels, we should honor authority, help and support our neighbors, love and honor our spouse, protect our neighbor's income, speak well of our neighbors, and help them keep what is theirs. It is rather that we need to say these matters in a new way in our time. We need to work for justice, hold each other person in respected dignity, treasure diversity, engage in empathy and compassionate regard, learn and treasure our own limits in power and possessions, resist consumerism, value our own vocations, rejoice in the wisdom of simplicity and the goodness of creation, care about the earth, and appropriately protest misused authority—we need to love our neighbor as ourselves.

The assembly forms us and sends us to these things. The catechism, those symbolic texts that come to us in our baptism, can be critically read to support this assembly.

Ignatius of Antioch, that early second-century martyr and bishop, helped me as I began this book by writing "I sing the assemblies." A more recent hymn writer has also done such singing. Huub Oosterhuis—a Dutch Roman Catholic priest and poet who was long pastor of a university-related assembly in Amsterdam and closely associated with the mid-twentieth-century renewal movement in the Netherlands—in 1968 published the hymn "Zomaar een dak boven wat hoofden," later translated into English as "What Is This Place." I have imagined this hymn as a brilliant choice when, after the pandemic absence, assemblies would begin to meet again. I also imagine it as a fine way for an assembly to refresh itself musically in its own identity from time to time. I am grateful to end this book—my own song of the assembly—with this hymn. A literal translation of the Dutch text might read,

> Just a roof above some heads,
> a door that stands open to silence,
> walls of skin, windows as eyes,
> traces toward hope and dawn,
> house that becomes a living body,
> when we go inside
> in order to stand before God.
>
> Words from afar, falling stars,
> sparks from the past sown here,
> names for God, dreams, signs,
> blown here from deep in the world,
> mouths of earth hear and see,
> remember, speak out,
> God's free and shining [or lifting] word.
>
> Table of one bread in order to know
> [or Table of One, bread in order to know]
> that we are given to each other,
> miracle of God, people in peace,
> old and forgotten new mystery,

breaking and sharing, being what cannot be,
doing what is unthinkable:
death and resurrection.

A full assembly can be heard and seen singing that hymn in Dutch, with heart and voice, by searching for "Zomaar en dak" on nederlandzingt .eo.nl. The tune is from a vigorous seventeenth-century Dutch song, "Komt Nu Met Zang."

The English translation of the hymn, excellently prepared by David Smith, was published in 1970. It can be found, among other places, as hymn 462 in Glory and Praise, 3rd ed. *(Oregon Catholic Press, 2015), hymn 404 in* Glory to God: The Presbyterian Hymnal *(Westminster John Knox, 2013), and hymn 524 in* Evangelical Lutheran Worship *(Augsburg Fortress, 2006):*

What is this place, where we are meeting?
Only a house, the earth its floor.
Walls and a roof, sheltering people,
windows for light, an open door.
Yet it becomes a body that lives
when we are gathered here,
and know our God is near.

Words from afar, stars that are falling,
sparks that are sown in us like seed:
names for our God, dreams, signs, and wonders
sent from the past are all we need.
We in this place remember and speak
again what we have heard:
God's free redeeming word.

And we accept bread at this table,
broken and shared, a living sign.
Here in this world, dying and living,
we are each other's bread and wine.
This is the place where we can receive
what we need to increase:
our justice and God's peace.

The hymn moves through the shape of the meeting. The Gathering is a bodily gathering in an ordinary, even humble place, but—as Luther said—"without place and body, there is no church." The house shelters the people. But even more, people and house together become a "body that lives" before God, a place where there are traces that point toward hope. The assembly is an event; it "becomes" that living body, Christ existing as congregation. Then the Word of God itself is remembered and spoken in and by the whole assembly, and it is full of seeds, sparks, stars, light, signs. That word is blown here or sent here from deep in the world and in the past; it is a deeply human, culturally rich thing. Yet it is, exactly at the same time, God's free, shining, redeeming word, coming here like stars falling from the sky. The assembly gathered around that Word is gathered around "names for our God" in a phrase that sounds like the positive use of the name commandment. And the Meal is a communal event, a living sign. It forms us into one another's bread and wine, making a people in peace and signing what cannot be: death and resurrection. Then while the original Dutch simply dwells in that "old and forgotten new mystery" enacted in the Meal, Christ's death and resurrection holding us all into life, the English translation draws out what is implied in both the "free redeeming word" and the Meal that gives us to one another. In the Sending, we know that this meeting has indeed provided us with "what we need to increase: our justice and God's peace." By the old and new mystery of death and resurrection, the assembly turns us toward our world and—like the Commandments—toward our neighbors.

Such is a spirituality of the assembly.

Ah, dear sheltering, needy, hopeful people: sing that assembly, be that assembly, with gratitude, humility, seriousness, and joy.

Works Cited

Below, listed by chapter, are works both quoted and consulted in the creation of that chapter. The books and articles are listed in the order in which reference to them occurs in the chapter. The following books were consulted throughout the work on this volume:

Kolb, Robert, and Timothy J. Wengert, eds., *The Book of Concord: The Confessions of the Evangelical Lutheran Church* (Minneapolis: Fortress, 2000).
Lathrop, Gordon W., *The Pastor: A Spirituality* (Minneapolis: Fortress, 2006).
———, *Holy People: A Liturgical Ecclesiology* (Minneapolis: Fortress, 1999).
Lathrop, Gordon W., and Timothy J. Wengert, *Christian Assembly: Marks of the Church in a Pluralistic Age* (Minneapolis: Fortress, 2004).

Preface

Lathrop, *Pastor*, 27.
Putnam, Robert D., *Bowling Alone: The Collapse and Revival of American Community* (New York: Simon and Schuster, 2000).
Rordorf, Willy, *Sabbat und Sontag in der Alten Kirche* (Zürich: Theologischer Verlag, 1972), 109. In the *Acts of the Martyrs of Abitina*, Emeritus is quoted as saying *sine dominico non possumus*. For a translation of part of the *Acts* see Lawrence J. Johnson, *Worship in the Early Church: An Anthology of Sources*, vol. 2 (Collegeville, MN: Liturgical Press, 2009), 1–2.

Hovda, Robert W., *Environment and Art in Catholic Worship* (Washington, DC: United States Catholic Conference, 1978), 18.

Watson, Nicholas, and Jacqueline Jenkins, *The Writings of Julian of Norwich* (University Park: Penn State University Press, 2006), 73.

Lake, Kirsopp, trans., "Epistles of Ignatius," in *The Apostolic Fathers*, vol. 1 (Cambridge, MA: Harvard University Press, 1959), 196–97 (translation slightly altered).

Introduction

The quotation from 1 Peter 2:9–10 is from *Readings for the Assembly, Cycle A* (Minneapolis: Augsburg Fortress, 1995), 174.

Bonhoeffer, Dietrich, *Sanctorum Communio: A Theological Study of the Sociology of the Church* (Minneapolis: Fortress, 1998), 121, 139, 141, 189–90.

Lathrop, *Pastor*, 4–5.

Williams, Rowan, *Christian Spirituality* (Atlanta: John Knox, 1979), 1–4.

Bonhoeffer, Dietrich, *Life Together and Prayerbook of the Bible* (Minneapolis: Fortress, 1996), 40–41, 43–44.

On the cantor as "leader of assembly song," see Chad Fothergill, *Sing with All the People of God: A Handbook for Church Musicians* (Minneapolis: Augsburg Fortress, 2020).

For the quotation from the martyr act about Emeritus, see Rordorf, *Sabbat und Sontag*, and Johnson, *Worship*, under sources for the preface.

Grundtvig, Nikolai, *Skal den Lutherske Reformation virkelig fortsættes?* (Copenhagen: Schauberg, 1863), 115–16; translated and quoted in Lathrop and Wengert, *Christian Assembly*, 50.

Chapter 1: What Is the Assembly?

For *ekklesiai* as "assemblies," see Gordon W. Lathrop, *Saving Images: The Presence of the Bible in Christian Liturgy* (Minneapolis: Fortress, 2017), 62–63.

Harland, Philip A., *Associations, Synagogues, and Congregations* (Minneapolis: Fortress, 2003).

Hays, Richard B., *The Conversion of the Imagination: Paul as Interpreter of Israel's Scripture* (Grand Rapids: Eerdmans, 2005), xv–xvi, 5–6.

Lake, Kirsopp, trans., *The Martyrdom of Polycarp*, initial inscription, in *The Apostolic Fathers*, vol. 2 (Cambridge, MA: Harvard University Press, 1959), 312–13.

Luther, Martin, "On the Councils and the Church," in *The Annotated Luther 3: Church and Sacraments*, ed. Paul W. Robinson (Minneapolis: Fortress, 2016), 422–31.

Evangelical Lutheran Church in America, *The Use of the Means of Grace: A Statement on the Practice of Word and Sacrament* (Minneapolis: Augsburg Fortress, 1997).

Calvin, John, *Institutes of the Christian Religion*, 1553 ed., trans. F. L. Battles (London: SCM, 1960), 4:17:44.

Hovda, *Environment and Art*, 22, 28–29. For further contemporary reflection on Hovda's understanding of assembly, especially its open and participatory character, see Bryan Cones, *This Assembly of Believers: Difference and Inclusion in the Church at Prayer* (London: SCM, 2020).

Chauvet, Louis-Marie, *The Sacraments: The Word of God at the Mercy of the Body* (Collegeville, MN: Liturgical Press, 2001), 34.

Hebert, A. G., "The Parish Communion in its Spiritual Aspect," in *The Parish Communion: A Book of Essays*, ed. A. G. Hebert (London: SPCK, 1937), 3.

For "assembly" among Orthodox, Old Catholic, and Reformed Churches, as well as in ecumenism generally, see Mattijs Ploeger, *Celebrating Church: Ecumenical Contributions to a Liturgical Ecclesiology* (Ridderkerk: Instituut voor Liturgievetenschap and Liturgisch Instituut, 2008).

Chapter 2: Why Is the Assembly Important?

For Bonhoeffer, *Sanctorum Communio*, see under sources for the introduction.

For Chauvet, *Sacraments*, see under sources for chapter 1.

Langer, Suzanne, *Philosophy in a New Key* (Cambridge, MA: Harvard University Press, 1978), 288–89.

Hopkins, Gerard Manley, "As Kingfishers Catch Fire," in *Poems*, ed. W. H. Gardner and N. H. Mackenzie, 4th ed. (London: Oxford University Press, 1967), 90.

Gaillardetz, Richard, *Transforming Our Days: Spirituality, Community and Liturgy in a Technological Age* (New York: Crossroad, 2000).

Putnam, Robert D., with Shaylyn Romney Garrett, *The Upswing: How America Came Together a Century Ago and How We Can Do It Again* (New York: Simon and Schuster, 2020).

On the differences between ritual and drama, see Roy A. Rappaport, *Ritual and Religion on the Making of Humanity* (Cambridge: Cambridge University Press, 1999), 39–42.

Francis, Bishop of Rome, *Fratelli Tutti: Encyclical Letter on Fraternity and Social Friendship* (October 3, 2020), 33, 43, 47.

On the dangers of an electronic representation of reality, see Nicholas Carr, *The Shallows: What the Internet Is Doing to Our Brains* (London: Atlantic Books, 2020).

Petriglieri, Gianpiero, "In Praise of the Office," *Harvard Business Review* (July 16, 2020).

Archytas of Tarentum is quoted in Joseph Leo Koerner, *The Reformation of the Image* (Chicago: University of Chicago Press, 2004), 80.

Chapter 3: Why Are the Sacraments Assembly Events?

For Bonhoeffer, *Sanctorum Communio*, see under sources for the introduction.

Evangelical Lutheran Church in America, *Use of the Means of Grace*, 20.

Evangelical Lutheran Worship (Minneapolis: Augsburg Fortress, 2006); for baptismal rite, see 227–31; on Vigil readings, see 269.

On biblical images for the eucharist, see Lathrop, *Saving Images*, 38–43.

Formula of Concord, in *Book of Concord*, ed. Kolb and Wengert, 607.

On the ministry of presiding, see Robert W. Hovda, *Strong, Loving, and Wise: Presiding in Liturgy* (Washington, DC: Liturgical Conference, 1976).

On "mutual conversation and consolation," see Martin Luther, *Smalcald Articles*, in *Book of Concord*, ed. Kolb and Wengert, 319.

For Chauvet, *Sacraments*, see under sources for chapter 1.

CHAPTER 4: HOW DOES THE ASSEMBLY FORM US FOR DAILY LIVING?

"Justin Martyr's Description of the Sunday Meeting," in Gordon W. Lathrop, *Central Things: Worship in Word and Sacrament* (Minneapolis: Augsburg Fortress, 2005), 79–80.

Common Worship: Services and Prayers for the Church of England (London: Church House, 2000), 183.

Evangelical Lutheran Worship, dismissals, 115.

Book of Common Worship (Louisville, KY: Westminster John Knox, 2018), 155.

Buchanan, Colin, ed., *Anglican Eucharistic Liturgies, 1985–2010* (Norwich: Canterbury Press, 2011), 76, 220.

Oslo City Mission dismissal translated in Ninna Edgardh, "Towards a Theology of Gathering and Sending," *Worship* 82, no. 6 (November 2008): 511–13.

Luther, Martin, "A Brief Instruction on What to Look for and Expect in the Gospels," in *The Annotated Luther 2: Word and Faith*, ed. Kirsi Stjerna (Minneapolis: Fortress, 2015), 32–33.

Evangelical Lutheran Worship, outline of intercessions, 105-6.

On thanksgiving and beseeching as forming a way to walk in the world, see Gordon W. Lathrop, "Walking on the Holy Ground: Liturgical Spirituality," in *Holy Ground: A Liturgical Cosmology* (Minneapolis: Fortress, 2003), 68–94.

Luther, Martin, "The Blessed Sacrament of the Holy and True Body of Christ, and the Brotherhoods," in *The Annotated Luther 1: The Roots of Reform*, ed. Timothy Wengert (Minneapolis: Fortress, 2015), 236, 241.

For the table prayer, see Gail Ramshaw, *Pray, Praise, and Give Thanks: A Collection of Litanies, Laments, and Thanksgivings at Font and Table* (Minneapolis: Augsburg Fortress, 2017), 41.

Luther, Martin, "The Babylonian Captivity of the Church," in *The Annotated Luther 3: Church and Sacraments*, ed. Paul Robinson (Minneapolis: Fortress, 2016), 47.

Luck bell inscription, in Lathrop, *Central Things*, 20.

Lojo Kyrka (Tavastehus, Finland: Lojo Församling, 1991).

Chapter 5: Catechism and Sacraments: The Purpose of Assembly

On lifelong study of the catechism and on the backward-forward reflection on the catechism, see Martin Luther, *The Large Catechism*, in *Book of Concord*, ed. Kolb and Wengert, 380, 431, 462.

Luther, Martin, *The Small Catechism*, in *Book of Concord*, ed. Kolb and Wengert, 347–64.

On the catechisms generally, see Timothy J. Wengert, *Martin Luther's Catechisms* (Minneapolis: Fortress, 2009).

On the origins of baptism and the Lord's Supper, see Gordon W. Lathrop, *The Four Gospels on Sunday* (Minneapolis: Fortress, 2012), 55–59, 171–73.

Bonhoeffer, *Life Together*, 44, 46, 110–11.

Luther, *Smalcald Articles*, in *Book of Concord*, ed. Kolb and Wengert, 319.

On the four Gospels, see Lathrop, *Saving Images*, 64–68.

On the ecumenical lectionary, see Gail Ramshaw, *Word of God, Word of Life: Understanding the Three-Year Lectionaries* (Minneapolis: Augsburg Fortress, 2019).

Chauvet, *Sacraments*, 34.

The Torslunde altar frontal can be seen in Lathrop and Wengert, *Christian Assembly*, 38.

Koerner, *Reformation of the Image*, 22.

Chapter 6: The Lord's Prayer: Assembly, Bread, and Forgiveness Now

The ecumenical translation of the Lord's Prayer is found in *Praying Together* (Boston: English Language Liturgical Consultation, 1988), 11–13.

One reconstruction of the earliest form of the Lord's Prayer is found in Joachim Jeremias, "The Lord's Prayer in the Light of Recent Research," in *The Prayers of Jesus* (Philadelphia: Fortress, 1978), 82–107.

For texts of the *Kaddish*, see *Authorized Daily Prayer Book of the United Hebrew Congregations of the British Commonwealth of Nations*, trans. S. Singer, 2nd ed. (London: Eyre and Spottiswoode, 1962), 15–16, 37–38, 78–81.

For a discussion of the *Kaddish*, see *Jewish Liturgy*, ed. Raphael Posner, Uri Kaploun, and Shalom Cohen (New York: Leon Amiel, 1975), 112–15.

Evangelical Lutheran Worship, Leaders Edition (Minneapolis: Augsburg Fortress, 2006), introduction to the Lord's Prayer, 206.

"Let the Vineyards Be Fruitful, Lord," *Lutheran Book of Worship* (Minneapolis: Augsburg, 1978), 66.

Ramshaw, *Pray, Praise, and Give Thanks*, 41.

The ikon of the Trinity can be seen in Leonid Ouspensky and Vladimir Lossky, *The Meaning of Icons* (Crestwood, NY: St. Vladimir's Seminary Press, 1982), 198.

Didascalia, in Lawrence J. Johnson, *Worship in the Early Church: An Anthology of Sources*, vol. 1 (Collegeville, MN: Liturgical Press, 2009), 233–34.

Chapter 7: The Creed: Assembly and the Communion of Saints

The ecumenical translations of the creeds are found in *Praying Together*, 16–24.

On the history of the creeds, see J. N. D. Kelly, *Early Christian Creeds* (London: Longman, 1981).

Evangelical Lutheran Worship; creeds and rubric, 104–5.
Luther, *Small Catechism*, in *Book of Concord*, ed. Kolb and Wengert, 354–56.
Lathrop, *Pastor*, 98–99.
Lake, *Martyrdom of Polycarp*, 312-313.
Bonhoeffer, *Life Together*, 44, 46.
Melanchthon, Philip, *Apology of the Augsburg Confession*, in *Book of Concord*, ed. Kolb and Wengert, 177.
Luther, Martin, "Against Caterinus," quoted in Koerner, *Reformation of the Image*, 411.
Lopez, Barry, *Arctic Dreams: Imagination and Desire in a Northern Landscape* (Toronto: Bantam, 1987), xx, 414.

Chapter 8: The Commandments: Assembly, the Name of God, and the Neighbor

Luther, *Small Catechism*, in *Book of Concord*, ed. Kolb and Wengert, 351–54.
Dr. Martin Luther's Small Catechism (St. Louis: Concordia, 1943), 5.
Evangelical Lutheran Worship, baptismal rite acclamation, 230; Thanksgiving at the Table X, 69; Psalm 95.
Ramshaw, *Pray, Praise, and Give Thanks*, 56.
Luther, "Blessed Sacrament," in *Annotated Luther 1*, 236.
———, "Against Caterinus," quoted in Koerner, *Reformation of the Image*, 411.
Texts from two hymns are included in this chapter:
Brokering, Herbert F., "Alleluia! Jesus Is Risen!," hymn 377 in *Evangelical Lutheran Worship*, stanza 3.
Oosterhuis, Huub, "What Is This Place," hymn 524 in *Evangelical Lutheran Worship*, stanzas 1–3. The literal translation from the original Dutch was prepared by the author of this volume.

Index

absolution, 58, 70
anointing the sick, 58, 71
assembly: in the Bible, 18–24; definition of, 1, 19, 24; paradoxes of, 5–9, 58, 68, 83; in theology and liturgy, 25–27
assembly song, 9, 24, 26, 28, 40, 87
Augsburg Confession, xi, 25

baptism, 58–63, 82–83 passim; origin of, 95–97
Bonhoeffer, Dietrich, 3, 8, 35, 60, 99, 129
book, 39–40
Borgman, Albert, 38
Brokering, Herbert, 149

catechism: definition of, 91; reading backward, 93–94, 120–21, 125–26; as symbolic texts, 11, 94, 116, 148
Catacombs of Priscilla, 31–32
Calvin, John, 26, 30, 69
Chauvet, Louis-Marie, 27, 28, 50, 71, 102
commandments, 135–46; numbering of, 138–39; reinterpretation of, 137–39
commemoration of the dead, 79, 130
commodification of sacraments, 39, 41, 57
communion of saints, 128–32

communities of trust, 42–44
creed, 92, 93, 119–33
critical studies, 91, 95, 105, 121, 137

Didascalia, 117
digital media, 44–45, 47–50
domestic church, 52, 85–86
drama, 45–46

ekklesia. See assembly
Emeritus, x, 12, 51, 140
English Language Liturgical Commission, 105, 107, 119–20
eschatology, 22, 96–98, 100, 107–10, 111–13
eucharist, 63–69, 81–82 passim; origin of, 95–98
eucharistic prayer, 56, 66, 67, 143–44

focal practices, 38–41, 48, 83, 143
Francis, Bishop of Rome, 47–48

Gaillardetz, Richard, 38
gestures, 31–32, 40
Grundtvig, Nicolai, 12–13

Hays, Richard, 21
Hebert, A. G., 27
Holy Spirit, 126–27 passim
house for assembly, 25, 30, 147–48
Hopkins, Gerard Manley, 37
Hovda, Robert, xi, 26–27, 28, 52, 133

Ignatius of Antioch, xii, 25, 147
image prohibition, 138–39
intercessions, 36, 39, 41, 79–80, 145

Julian of Norwich, xii, 25
Justin Martyr, 28, 74, 78–79

Kaddish, 107–9, 114
keys, office of the, 98–100, 112
Koerner, Joseph Leo, 104

Langer, Suzanne, 36
lectionary, 29, 52, 85–86, 102
liturgy, 10–11 passim
Lohja church, 87–88
Lopez, Barry, 133–34
Lord's Prayer, 30, 105–17; ecclesiology of, 110–13; theology of, 113–16
luck bell, 87–88
Luther, Martin, 25–26, 77–78, 81–82, 86, 123–25, 133, 139–42

marriage, 71, 143
marks of the church, 25–26, 30, 132, 133
Martyrdom of Polycarp, 23, 128
material reality, 44–48
Melanchthon, Philip, 25, 133
metaphor, 41, 60, 65, 83, 143
ministries in assembly, 9, 67
music. *See* assembly song

name of God, 142–45, 149
neighbor love, 77–78, 81–82, 145–46

Oosterhuis, Huub, 147–49
orans posture, 31–32, 40, 56

ordination, 58, 70, 143
ordo, fourfold, 29, 74 passim; Gathering, 17–18; Meal, 55–56; Sending, 73–74; Word, 33–34

pandemic, ix–x, 46, 48–49, 52, 61, 64, 84–87, 112
paschal candle, 13, 143
Paul, 2–3, 18–20, 21–24, 28, 95–96, 131
Petriglieri, Gianpiero, 51
presiding, 28, 66
Putnam, Robert, ix–x, 42

qahal, 21, 22, 107

rituals, 36–41
Rublev, Andrei, 118

sabbath, 140–42
sacramental word, 100–102
service, 10
spirituality, definition of, 5–6
song. *See* assembly song
symbol, 36 passim; assembly as, 2–4, 10, 37; broken, 3–4; catechism as, 11, 94, 116, 146; creed as, 92, 122; definition of, 2

Torslunde altar frontal, 102–3
Trinity, 9, 22, 114, 116, 124–25 passim

Williams, Rowan, 6
Wittenberg altarpiece, xi, 103
worship, 10